somewhere to hang my nat

To Toni,
Our dear friend.
With fondest love
from

Dorsune & Ian

Stanley Price's grandparents all came from Lithuania to Ireland. His parents were born in Dublin and much of his early life was divided between Dublin and London. An equally divided education ended up at Cambridge University where he read History. He went on to work as a journalist in New York and London before he became a full-time writer. He has written four novels and numerous plays for the theatre and television. He now lives in London with his wife and they spend as much time as possible in Ireland.

Also by Stanley Price

Novels
Crusading for Kronk
A World of Difference
Just for the Record
The Biggest Picture

Plays
Horizontal Hold
The Starving Rich
The Two of Me
Moving
Why Me?

(For television)
All Things Being Equal
Star Quality
Close Relations
Genghis Cohn
A Royal Scandal

SOMEWHERE TO HANG MY HAT

An Irish–Jewish Journey

STANLEY PRICE

NEW ISLAND

SOMEWHERE TO HANG MY HAT
An Irish–Jewish Journey
First published November 2002
by New Island
2 Brookside
Dundrum Road
Dublin 14

ISBN 1 902602 90 0

New Island receives financial assistance from The Arts Council
(An Chomhairle Ealaíon), Dublin, Ireland.

Jacket design: Sin É Design
Printed in Ireland by Colour Books Ltd.

1 3 5 4 2

CONTENTS

To Judy and Munro

1. Departure

London 1972

After forty years of living and working in England, he still had his soft Dublin accent, but his voice was much weaker now. He looked very frail, his face white and pinched. As he lay back on the pillows, the black *yamulkah* on his head was pathetically askew. It was an effort for him to speak – "You were always a Communist, even when you were at Oxford." He shut his eyes and drifted off into sleep. These were the last words my father spoke to me.

I had never been a Communist in my life, and I had never been at Oxford. At the end, the increasing shots of morphine had confused him. It was my brother Ashley who had been at Oxford, and what I had always been was not a Communist, but a Bolshie. My father should have remembered that – he was responsible.

I went home, where the phone rang around midnight. It was the night nurse, advising me to come over quickly as my father was fading very fast. She said that she hadn't awakened my mother who was asleep in another room.

Ashley had already arrived when I got there and was sending the night nurse home. My father had died a few minutes before. Even though we had expected his end for some days, the finality of it still came as a shock. All I remember of that moment was the sadness that he had died thinking me an Oxford Communist.

"I'd better go in … and see him," I said.

"Have you ever seen a dead body before?" my brother asked.
"No," I said.

"I wouldn't if I was you. He doesn't look too good."

I felt relieved not to have to go into the bedroom. I was also touched that my brother was trying to spare me a painful experience. Now I would remember our father as he was when he was alive.

I am eight years older than Ashley. I was married, he was not, which I felt at the time was partially my fault. He was a doctor, so it felt right that he should be in charge. Then we remembered the Jewish tradition that a dead body must not be left alone. While the soul makes its journey from this world to the next, someone must be there to guard against an evil spirit taking possession of the body. Orthodox communities employ people to sit with the dead before burial. At two in the morning we were not going to find anyone, even if we had known who to call.

"We could take it in turns to sit in there," I said, knowing I sounded less than enthusiastic. It was a small flat, with the main bedroom just off the living-room. My brother and I agreed that if we left the door open and one of us stayed awake, no evil spirit could sneak past us. We sat there, talking, sleeping in turns, our mother asleep in one bedroom, our father dead in the other. I don't remember much of the conversation, except talking about Ireland and "dirty, old Dublin" as my mother affectionately called it. Our father had always wanted to end up there, not in London. As an Irishman and a Jew, he had lived in a double diaspora. Now, a long-time exile, he had died away from home.

When someone close to you dies after a long and painful illness, the initial feeling, much as one may not want to admit it, is one of relief. The sense of loss only strikes later. The grief for my father had hit six months earlier. The consultant had told us that the bladder cancer they had kept in check for some years had finally spread and was now terminal. Desolated, I walked round and round the block outside the hospital in the dark, trying to think of some prayer that would bring consolation. Nothing came – in English or in Hebrew. Only some lines from *Hamlet*, learned at school, which kept going through my head like some mourning mantra: "But you must know your father lost a father; that father lost, lost his …" I couldn't remember the rest. I looked it up later; it was Claudius to Hamlet: "… that father lost, lost his; and the survivor bound in filial obligation for some term to do obsequious sorrow." I discovered that "obsequious" had two meanings in the dictionary, funereal or fawning. There was nothing fawning about my sorrow, but the idea of nature taking its course through the generations brought some perspective and consolation. There had been four years when my father and I were alienated from each other, and out of touch. After the reconciliation, our relationship had become warmer and closer than before. I now longed to have those four lost years back.

A doctor himself, he must have known for some time that his death was imminent. He had clearly made the decision not to mention it to anyone in the family. As his end grew near, his prayer book was increasingly in evidence. Despite all his efforts, he had signally failed to pass on his religious faith to me, but I was glad it was a comfort to him.

My father had also wanted me to follow in his professional, as well as his religious, footsteps. There too he had failed. When I had consistently got the worst marks in the class for chemistry and physics, he had said that didn't matter. He claimed that if you put your mind to it, these subjects could be mastered. And when I pleaded unutterable squeamishness, he insisted that didn't matter either. Only the first couple of anatomy lessons might be difficult. He had thrown up once, and that was that. When I said that I really wanted to be a writer, he said grand, but become a doctor first – look at Cronin, Maugham, Chekhov. I was never to follow in their medical footsteps. And I was to disappoint my father in other ways too.

Ashley was good at physics and chemistry and utterly

unsqueamish. He duly became a doctor. It seemed appropriate the night my father passed away that we should sit up together in my parents' living-room, doors open against evil spirits, with Ashley acting as protector of my delicate artistic sensibilities. Only later did I feel ashamed about being so squeamish and finally found an occasion on which to make up for it.

In the morning we broke the news to our mother. Normally a highly emotional woman, she took it better than we had expected. Everything else now became a blur of frantic activity. According to Jewish law, a body must be buried within thirty-six hours. Urgent phone calls were made to the Celtic fringes of our small family. Virtually all of our close family still lived in Dublin. Only my mother's sister Muriel and her husband Jack lived in Glasgow. There were also the members of that strange, recondite group, the Irish–Jewish Graduates Association. That might sound like half-a-dozen phone calls. How many people could have such particular and esoteric qualifications? In fact, well over a hundred, enough to hold their annual dinner-dance at a big West End hotel. As my father had once been a reluctant chairman, the entire membership could be expected at the funeral and afterwards. The run on whiskey would be considerable.

What we dreaded most was the arrival of "The Girls". The Girls was my father's euphemism for his two spinster sisters in Dublin, both now well into their seventies. Two less girlish figures it would be hard to imagine. My mother always said they looked "as if they'd come out of the Ark". It was hard to imagine when they had last bought clothes, let alone where. As a child in Dublin, their clumpy shoes had always reminded me of Minnie Mouse. Oddly enough, one was actually called Minnie, the other Hilda. They still lived in the run-down, terraced, family-house on the South Circular Road at Dolphin's Barn, the heart of what used to be called "Little Jerusalem", a name bestowed by a native who no doubt thought he was being witty rather than anti-Semitic.

My father lived in terror of The Girls. It was, I suspected, a terror based on guilt. He had escaped from the small, claustrophobic home and found a profession and a wife. They stayed behind, unmarried, unloved, looking after an invalid mother, going out two or three times a week in a ramshackle old Ford Prefect to collect the payments on the small items of domestic goods that they sold. They were, in fact, what used to be called "tally-men", in Yiddish a *Veekele*, a weekly collector, the forerunners of hire purchase. Professionally, they were following in the footsteps of their father, my grandfather, Charles Beresford Price.

The profit from these labours obviously fell somewhat short of making ends meet, and they saw it as my father's fraternal duty to bring these ends into closer union. They wrote him a weekly letter that invariably came on a Friday morning. An unvarying ritual attended the arrival of the letter. My father never needed to see the handwriting on the envelope, or the Irish stamp, as he had a sixth sense for their letter like a diviner for water. In any pile of letters, theirs was the one he totally ignored, acting as though it were invisible. After he finished his breakfast and went off to the surgery, my mother would clear the table, pick up the unopened letter, and invariably say, "I do wish they wouldn't write and upset him." She would then put the unopened letter on the mantelpiece in the breakfast-room.

There is an injunction forbidding the cutting of paper or cloth on the Sabbath. My father thus had a religious sanction for not opening the letter for a further twenty-five hours, from the arrival of the Sabbath, an hour before sunset on Friday evening, till sunset on Saturday, when I would see him hovering round the mantelpiece, his face peaky with anxiety. Suddenly lunging at the letter, he would open it and glare at the couple of pages for a few moments. And that was it – he never read the letters properly. There was no need – the contents were unchanging. I know, because I inherited the letters and the ritual. In my case, though, the letters arrived on a monthly rather than a weekly basis.

Conveying the news of my father's death to The Girls was neither easy, nor cheap. They had never had a phone in their house, so one had to phone their neighbour, an elderly lady whom Ashley and I had come to call "the sainted Mrs Quirke". She was in her sixties, and agoraphobic, so getting her to go next door wasn't easy at the best of times. I was never very clear what terrible things could happen to her in transit between 187 and 189 South Circular Road. The IRA had never been in the habit of kidnapping elderly, widowed Catholic ladies for ransom. To be knocked down by a car on the pavement would have taken some very drunken driving, even by Dublin standards. This time it was easier. I had only to say "Hello, Mrs Quirke. I'm afraid I've got some rather bad news for …" for her to say "Ah, the poor man! He's dead so." From previous experience, I had learned that most of Mrs Quirke's sentences ended in "so", a sort of Irish full stop. "I'll go and fetch her so."

Not a fast mover, Mrs Quirke would first have to put on her walking shoes and coat before risking the great outdoors. I knew it would be Hilda whom she would fetch. She was marginally the younger of the sisters, and the relationship between the pair was based on a perfect compatibility. Hilda did everything, Minnie did nothing. Then more time would pass while Hilda made herself look respectable before venturing out to her neighbour's house. There was another complication – Hilda was fairly deaf. It isn't easy to break bad news gently at the top of one's voice. After the third time of shouting "Dad's died," she got the message. There was a long silence before Mrs Quirke came back on the phone and said "Hilda's very upset." I asked her to explain that the funeral had to be tomorrow, Thursday, and that a Dublin – London flight for the following morning had been booked and paid for.

I could hear Mrs Quirke shouting these details to Hilda, and a lot of incoherent shouting back. By now the cost of the phone call had eaten substantially into whatever small legacy my father had left. Mrs Quirke eventually came back to the phone. "They've never been up in an airplane before. They don't want to fly so." I made her relay to Hilda that if they came by boat and train they would miss the funeral, that planes were now safer than boats. I would meet them at the airport. Eventually, with Mrs Quirke as shrieking intermediary, Hilda agreed. With money no longer any object, I thanked the sainted Mrs Quirke profusely. By now she had forgotten who was deaf and who wasn't. She screamed back down the phone "Ah sure, God bless you, it was the least I could do so."

Next day I went to Heathrow to meet The Girls. As they came out of Customs into the arrivals lounge, they indeed looked as if they came from another age. If not "off the Ark", certainly not off an Aer Lingus jet. They came towards me, two sad, stooping little figures, totally lost in the vastness of the airport. They had clearly, in their combined terror and grief, been crying. They looked relieved to see me. I tried to be cheerful. "What do you think of flying then?" I asked. Minnie said nothing. Hilda said "What?" I repeated the question several decibels louder. Hilda said "What?" I tried again. Hilda shook her head, "The flying's made me deaf."

I drove them to my parents' flat, where I was met by an undertaker with a pair of scissors. I had been warned to wear something old, as cutting the next of kin's clothing was a sign of mourning. I gestured at my old black tie. He cut it in half. The coffin was then carried out of the flat. There was a greater finality attached to this than what would happen later at the cemetery. This was my father leaving home forever. We now proceeded to the United Synagogue's cemetery at Bushey, where a majority of London's Jews have been buried, only inches apart, for the past seventy years. Ashley meanwhile had to drive there via Euston to collect Aunt Muriel and Uncle Jack from Glasgow. We had begged them to fly down the day before to keep my mother company. They said they couldn't arrange a flight that quickly. I wasn't sure I believed them.

A Jewish funeral is impressive for its starkness and simplicity. The chapel is unadorned, and there are no seats. The prayers are brief. The coffin, of plain wood with a minimum of adornment, is wheeled to the grave on a bare, sideless, wooden cart. In the chapel, and beside the grave, the male next-of-kin recite the prayer for the dead, *Kaddish*. Like everyone of my generation brought up in orthodoxy, I had learned to read and recite classical Hebrew. It was taught basically for the purposes of prayer and ritual, not as a language, in much the same way as Catholics learned Latin. Understood or not, the words and rhythms of the *Kaddish* have an almost hypnotic power to summon up a sort of race-memory of loss and grief.

There must have been close to a hundred people at the funeral. Their accents were predominantly Irish, and now, according to tradition, everyone was heading for my parents' flat for tea or something stronger and a brief service led by the local rabbi – everyone except Uncle Jack and Auntie Muriel that is. They were, by our standards, rolling in money, but they were on cheap day-returns from Glasgow and were scared of missing their train back. Ashley, in a fury, had to drive them straight back to Euston. As he slammed his car door on them in the car-park, he hissed at me, "Bloody Scots Jews!"

Both Ashley and I had long given up any orthodox Jewish observance by this stage in our lives, but we still sat *Shiva* for the full week. During *Shiva* the chief mourners are expected not to go to work, to attend the morning prayers at the synagogue, and to have prayers in the home every evening, where the mourners sit on low chairs, and family and friends come to offer their condolences. The mourners don't shave, have their hair cut, or listen to music or any other entertainment. Our mother and The Girls, who were extremely orthodox, expected this of us, and it was what our father would have wanted. I had always been in awe of his extraordinary self-discipline about religious observance. Our week's *Shiva* fell well short of his own observance of the orthodox period of mourning. His entailed not just a week, but a full year of attendance at morning and evening synagogue services, and avoidance of any public or private entertainment. His father had died in 1940, his only brother in 1945, and his mother in 1946. He had thus been in this purdah of mourning for three years out of six, and during most of this period he was also coping with being an over-worked doctor in wartime London. My mother, by no means as devout, had, despite occasional protest, gone along with it.

Keeping to this routine for a week was suprisingly comforting, however. In the evenings, people came to the flat for a brief service taken by the local rabbi. By coincidence, he too was from Dublin, a theological firebrand known as "Blazes" Bernstein, with a reputation as an appalling driver – a reputation he confirmed by reversing into a visiting mourner's car in the car-park of my parents' flat. After the prayers my mother, Ashley, and The Girls sat in a row on our small chairs. It never reached the heights of a purely Irish wake, but endless tea and whiskey was poured. People crouched down beside us to tell us how much they had loved our father – as a friend, as a doctor, as a cousin, as an erratic bridge-partner, as a hopeless golfer, as a good Jew, as a patriotic Irishman. More than anything else they remembered his infectious laugh. He didn't tell jokes particularly well, and frequently never finished them, as the mere prospect of the punch line would start him laughing before he got there. Once he started laughing the effect was irresistible, the punch line having become irrelevant.

Initially I was embarrassed at having to go to the synagogue at 7.30, before breakfast, to recite the required *Kaddish*. The other, more devout early-risers – there had to be ten adults, a *minyan*, for a service to be held – would surely notice that Ashley and I had not been of their company for a good many years. If they did notice, they were tactful about it, no doubt used to mourners of lapsed faith. Some skills, like swimming and cycling, once learned are never forgotten. Fortunately, putting on phalacteries, *tefillim*, and praying in Hebrew are among them.

Every morning "Blazes" Bernstein was there, and at one service he caused us probably the most embarrassing experience of our lives. It was the custom that twice a week the service was extended to allow the rabbi to exhibit his learning. This took the form of a recitation, mainly in English, from the Talmud, the rabbinical commentaries on the Pentateuch, or the *Shulchan Aruch*, a 15th-century compilation of the rules that govern Jewish law and life. Traditionally the rabbi intersperses these texts with his own comments on the commentary. It is dialectical hair-splitting of mind-boggling intensity. That morning Rabbi Bernstein had chosen, for reasons best known to himself, a section from the *Shulchan Aruch* about certain problems of personal hygiene pertaining to the saying of one's prayers – particularly the *Amidah*.

The *Amidah* is the most sacred prayer of any service, and is recited standing to attention and facing east, towards Jerusalem. According to Rabbi Bernstein, the text was particularly concerned that anyone needing to go to the toilet should do so before commencing to say the *Amidah*. What should happen though if you didn't need to go when you started, but the urge occurred during the prayer? Seemingly you should not move but try to finish the prayer before going. Fair enough, but then Rabbi Bernstein launched into more subtle matters. What should you do if you stood up to say the *Amidah* and your neighbour broke wind? This weighty problem seemed to revolve around which was the greater sin – to move while reciting the *Amidah*, or to stay put and pray on in the midst of a foul odour? The answer was that you moved if you could, but if you couldn't, rather than disturb your neighbour, you stopped and waited for the odour to disperse before finishing the prayer. For added surrealism, Rabbi Bernstein intoned all this in the traditional, Rabbinical singsong, only overlaid with his Irish accent. It was Sholom Alecheim out of Samuel Beckett.

By now Ashley and I were into convulsive, suppressed giggles, but Rabbi Bernstein was to give us no quarter. The *Shulchan Aruch* had more hairs to split. What if you were praying privately and in the midst of the *Amidah* you involuntarily broke wind yourself? Rabbi Bernstein looked up as though waiting for a bright boy in the class to offer the answer. There was total silence – not a breath of anything. The answer itself was straightforward – you step back four cubits, wait until the odour ceases, return to the original place, and say a special prayer, something about your shame and embarrassment, before recommencing the *Amidah*. I can't remember how Bernstein rounded off his scatological *tour de force* because, by now, our silent giggles had turned into painfully repressed hysteria. We tried not to listen to any more for fear of being carried, quivering and helpless, out of the synagogue and straight into hospital.

There was a silence. Rabbi Bernstein had finished. My neighbour nudged me. To my horror I realised that this was a point where we were expected to recite the *Kaddish* again. Ashley was shaking like a jelly. We stood up, trying desperately to control ourselves. We started off together, but my voice began trembling, and I stopped. It was humiliating. My father not dead a week, and the others would now see me shaking with laughter, mocking their devotions and his memory. Ashley ploughed on courageously, as quavery-voiced I made a superhuman effort to join him. My voice was strangled, the tears now spilling down my cheeks. I prayed, not for my father's soul, but that the other congregants might see my tears only as a sign of filial distress. Somehow we made it to the end. A few minutes later, in the safety of our car, we collapsed in a howling heap. Thanks to my tears, I couldn't see to put the key into the ignition. And it was ten minutes before I had recovered enough to drive the car.

Unshaven, in deep mourning, I had laughed uncontrollably in a synagogue. I should have felt guilty, but I didn't. Instead I had a sense of relief, almost of achievement. I had finally gone into a synagogue of my own volition, and on my own terms. The service had lasted half an hour. I had said the requisite prayers out of respect for my father, and that was that. All my previous experiences of synagogue attendance had been no laughing matter. The average Saturday morning service lasts three hours. In my early teens those hours crawled by in excruciating boredom. There I was, unmanly in my *yamulkah* and prayer shawl, while gilded Aryan youth was out playing away games for the 1st XV. The rigid orthodoxy, imposed by my father, was oppressive, and by the time I was fifteen, we were at constant theological loggerheads. We argued bitterly about the dead hand of tradition, about why an egalitarian God would want a chosen people, and if He did, why was He so neurotically concerned about what they ate? In my father's eyes, I became a Bolshie, an apostate, a race traitor.

Inevitably there were business matters to attend to in that week of *Shiva*, papers to be sorted, financial muddle to be untangled. It was occupational therapy, and I tried to enlist my mother to take her mind off her grief. In one of my father's drawers there was a box of family souvenirs. Among them was a theatre programme for my first play, produced some five years before. My parents and brother had come to the first night of its short, but happy, life in the West End. Afterwards we had all stood together under the marquee. My mother looked up at what was surely a mother's dream – her son's name in lights – and she said, actually said, "Please God, it should lead to something." At that moment she attained the apotheosis of Jewish motherhood. Only afterwards did I work out the full sub-text – having your name in lights on one theatre is but a beginning, a small first step on the long journey to having your name simultaneously on all the marquees in town.

The design on the programme cover incorporated the two masks of Greek drama, comedy, with its mouth turned upward, and tragedy with its mouth turned down. It struck me that they perfectly symbolised my father's strange, divided nature. The mask with the upturned mouth was the jovial, gregarious Irishman, red-faced, infectious laugh at the ready. The mask with the down-turned mouth was the serious, religious Jew, obsessive about minute observances, his face pale and anxious when confronted by sisterly complaint or filial rebellion. And I had grown up in their twin presence, comic Irish, tragic Jewish, long before I knew they were the masks of classical drama.

Shiva ended. As I drove The Girls back to Heathrow, I realised they would now be our responsibility, as would our mother, already drifting into depression. I felt a shameful twinge of anger at my father. He had gone and left me in the lurch. As they left, The Girls said they hoped that I would continue saying *Kaddish* in synagogue if not for the full year, at least for a month. I said "Of course," then watched them disappear forlornly into the departure lounge, en route back to their lonely, impoverished life together on Dublin's South Circular Road.

1972 was a black year all round. It had started with my having a play on tour that failed to find a West End home. Recovering from the disappointment on a holiday in France, we had a car accident. My wife, Judy, broke several ribs and damaged two vertebrae. Our nine-year-old son and I escaped with minor cuts and bruises. We sued the other driver, whom we believed totally responsible, and four years later were awarded a modest sum for damages in a French court.

We returned home after that accident to find my father hadn't long to live. Judy's back mended slowly. Our front door, meanwhile, had warped so malignly that it had to be firmly banged shut. After my father's death, creeping out early to go to synagogue one morning, I didn't bang the door hard enough. Our dog got out for a solo morning trot and was killed by a large lorry on a nearby main road. For weeks afterwards whenever we found a dog-hair on a chair, or in the car, it would act as a trigger, and we would weep inconsolably. Yet we realised that only a small proportion of our tears were for the poor dog.

2. Arrival

While we sat *Shiva* a fair proportion of the people who came to commiserate and pray were, inevitably, Irish Jews, the men nearly all doctors or dentists, first generation Irish-born Jews. Whereas their parents still regarded Russia as "*der heim*", my parents and their circle regarded Dublin, Cork or Limerick as "home".

When they originally came to work in London, my parents were suspicious of their neighbours for being neither Jewish nor Irish. The two peoples with the largest diasporas are the Irish and the Jews, so to be an Irish Jew was to suffer a double diaspora. My parents and their friends overcame any drawback this posed by convincing themselves that Irish Jews were superior in taste and temperament to English Jews of whatever origin. They created the equivalent of an Irish-Jewish ghetto in London. Since they had gone where the work was, it was an ethnic and cultural, rather than a geographic, ghetto. These mourners were the people who were my parents' closest friends. They had trooped in and out of our house in London since I was a child. They played golf and bridge together, went to the races, and cheered for Ireland at rugby, the only game at which the Irish seemed to be on a parity with the English. Scattered mostly round London, with a few in Liverpool or Manchester, they were in constant touch by telephone, exchanging medical advice and racing tips. After thirty-odd years in England their Irish accents were as intact as their nicknames – Joxer, the General, Sir James, Chocolate, Gink, Matty. My early life alternated between this tight little community in London and the family still back in the real Ireland. If *heim* is where the heart is, I was never quite sure of the location of either. A fashionable identity problem was guaranteed.

In retrospect, I realise that I had mixed in London only with my parents' generation of Irish Jews, men and women in their forties and early fifties, an exiled professional middle class. Back in Dublin, I mixed with their parents. I still have memories of many of them, men and women in their sixties and seventies, who had come to Ireland in the 1880s and 1890s, refugees from Czarist oppression. They had strange accents when they spoke English. I didn't realise at the time what a unique mixture it was – Russian-Irish-English – nor how they nearly all came from a cluster of small villages in what is now Lithuania. But these were by no means the first Jews to arrive. The Wandering Jew had not forgotten Ireland.

The Irish Jewish Museum in Walworth Road, Dublin, was opened in 1985 by Chaim Hertzog, the President of Israel, born in Belfast, and brought up in Dublin where his father was Chief Rabbi. The first exhibit in the Museum is an extract from the *Annals of Innisfallen* dated 1079. It records that "Five Jews came over the sea with gifts for the Tairdelbach, King of Munster and they were sent back again." There is no record of where the five Jews were sent back to, or what happened to the gifts.

The Museum has little pre-19th-century material in its archive, but there is a record of a Jewish Mayor of Youghal, William Annyas, in 1555. Annyas was a Spanish Marrano, one of those Jews forced by the Inquisition to renounce their religion and accept baptism. Many practised their religion secretly. The family came to live in London. A nephew, Francis, acted as a spy for Sir Francis Drake in the Azores and served in the garrison in Youghal, where he, in turn, became Mayor.

When Cromwell in the 1650s allowed Jews back into England after 300 years, a few spilled over into Ireland. There is a record of three Portuguese Jews, two by name of Pereira, taking up residence in Dublin in 1660 and becoming prosperous merchants. Around this same time, there being no agreement about the date, a synagogue of no more than a couple of rooms was founded in Crane Lane, an alleyway between Dame Street and the Liffey. Another Pereira was William III's quartermaster at the Battle of the Boyne and appears to have subsequently settled in Dublin. A further Sephardic trickle followed, and in 1703 there are records of land being acquired on lease for a Jewish cemetery at Ballybough on the outskirts of Dublin, previously used as a graveyard for suicides. Forty years later, the cemetery's lease was extended for a thousand years for £34 10s, at a rent of one peppercorn per annum. For the rest of the 18th century the size of the Jewish community in Ireland fluctuated, but it never numbered more than 200 individuals, mostly living in Dublin. These were mainly merchants in import and export, and in trade as goldsmiths, silversmiths, and watchmakers. There is also a record of a synagogue in a house on Marlborough Street, adjacent to where the Abbey Theatre is today.

With the growth of newspapers and periodicals, it becomes easier to trace the ebb and flow of the always tiny Jewish community. In *The Dublin Evening Post* for 26th May, 1733, there is a reference to a Jew named Abraham Judah at Trinity College:

> On Monday last between 11 o'clock in the morn-
> ing and two in the afternoon, a conference was
> held between Mr Abraham Judah, Teacher of the
> Hebrew Language in Trinity College, and Mr
> Christian Fandy, a person who pretends to the
> same, at the public Library of St Sepulchre's in the
> presence of the Rev. Doctor Sheridan and the Rev.
> John Alexander, and several other gentlemen
> skilled in the language, in which meeting
> sufficient Proof were given of the before-
> mentioned Christian Fandy's inability to teach

either the pure Hebrew or any of the Rabbinical Writings, notwithstanding his mighty pretensions. At which time, on the other hand, Mr Abraham Judah was much applauded for the understanding which he showed upon the Occasion.

It appears that the conference was convened after the aforementioned Mr Christian Fandy published proposals for printing a grammar in Hebrew and selling it by advance subscriptions. Clearly the competitive oral exam in Hebrew between Messrs Judah and Fandy had exposed the latter as a fraud. Yet fraudulent or not, it does suggest that there was enough contemporary interest in Hebrew, as the language of the Bible, to make advertising a Hebrew grammar a worthwhile proposition. A year later an advertisement appeared in *Hamiltons Dublin Advertiser*:

> Proposals for Printing by Subscription, a new Hebrew Grammar, Compiled by Abraham Judah, Teacher of Hebrew in Trinity College, Dublin. Subscriptions are taken by Joseph Leathley, Abraham Bradley, and Thomas Moor, Booksellers in Dames Street, Thomas Thornton, Booksellers in College Green, and by the Author himself at Trinity College.
>
> N.B. The Author will attend any Gentleman who has a desire to learn the Pure or Rabbinical Hebrew or Comments on the Bible by Rabbi Solomon Yerachi, Rabbi Levi ben Gershein, Rabbi Moses Bar Nachman, etc.

These "Comments on the Bible" by a list of rabbis are, of course, the Talmud. Clearly Abraham Judah didn't use that word for fear that no one would know it, but he must have been optimistic that he would find takers for his private tuition in the subject. I only wonder if a generation of earnest 18th-century Irish Talmudic scholars would have collapsed in hysterical heaps as the rabbis discoursed, via Mr Judah, on the correct reaction to one's neighbour breaking wind at solemn moments?

The following advertisement appeared in *Reillys Dublin News Letter* of 30th December, 1738:

> The Jew's Musick is to be had at the Sign of the Fiddle and Dulcimer in Copper Alley, by Archibald Williamson, whom Gentlemen are pleased to call the IRISH JEW.
> N.B. Said Williamson provides Bands of Musick for private Balls, etc.

From the same paper for 31st May, 1740:

> London. May 22. Yesterday died in St Mary's Ax, Mr Francis Pereira, a noted Jew of Change Alley, worth £100,000.

One must assume that an announcement of this particular death in London appeared in a Dublin paper because Francis Pereira was one of the Irish-Jewish-Portuguese Pereiras who had settled in Dublin eighty years before. To have amassed £100,000 (well over £50 million by today's standards) shows considerable enterprise. Another interesting death was announced in *Scots Magazine*:

> Moses Jacob Cowan, the little Polander, 2 feet high, born in Polish Prussia, died in Dublin, Feb. 16th, 1748, aged 65.

A large crowd, drawn to see his tiny coffin, was reported to have attended the funeral at Ballybough Jewish Cemetery.

In 1746, there were estimated to be 40 Jewish families, around 200 individuals, living in Dublin, and clearly some were wealthy. There were more to come. On 3rd October, 1747, *Faulkners Journal* reported:

> Last week some Jew Merchants of great wealth arrived here from Holland in order to settle in Ireland.

The same journal, on 11th November, 1752, contained the announcement:

> Just arrived from London, Jacob Hymes and Henry Jacob, in Co., at the Sign of the Bull's Head, Bachelor's Walk, who make and sell all sorts of Black and Red Pencils by wholesale, cedar and cane, at the lowest Profit. They will take back any pencils that do not answer the Expectations of the Buyer; and as they intend settling here, hope for the Encouragement of the Public.

The arrival of Jewish merchants like these in the mid-18th century is proof of the political stability and economic growth of Dublin which was by then the second city of the British Empire in population, and the fifth in Europe. Under the Anglican supremacy, however, Jews suffered from much the same civil disabilities as Catholic and Protestant dissenters. As in England, Jews were limited to various manufacturing trades and financial undertakings, but in Ireland there was at least a strong political movement to emancipate them. Between 1743 and 1780 four different Bills to give Jews greater civil rights were presented in the Irish Parliament, although all narrowly failed. It was this failure, together with the general political unrest and economic recession in the 1780s–90s, that led to the decline of the Jewish community by the end of the century.

In 1818 it is recorded that for a time only two Jewish families were still living in Dublin, the Phillips and the Cohens. A contemporary history of the city of Dublin actually describes them:

> Their features and persons bear the indelible marks of their nation. Several efforts have been made to convert them without success; they are honest, harmless people.

The Phillips were grocers, the Cohens pencil-makers. There is no record of what happened to Hymes and Jacob who had advertised their "Black and Red Pencils" in *Faulkners Dublin Journal* of November, 1752. Their pencils seem to have no connection with the Cohens, whose Barnaby is credited with having introduced the graphite lead pencil into Ireland in 1795. With his brother, Abraham, Barnaby founded the company of B & J Cohen, who successfully marketed their pencils at a halfpenny each. Even then the Irish had their penchant for nicknames – Barnaby being known as "Pencil" Cohen and his brother Abraham as "Miser" Cohen. The latter's obituary merited a whole column in a fashionable London periodical, *The Gentlemans Magazine*, of March 1854:

> At Dublin, a Jew named Cohen who followed the trade of pencil-maker. Although living to outward appearances in a state of wretchedness, he was known to be possessed of wealth and it is believed that the sum will prove to be not under, if not above £60,000. A brother of Baron Rothschild is an executor of the will.

To have made that much out of pencils surely proves that even in those days the Irish were a nation of scribblers.

In fact, the actual sum turned out to be £45,000, yet still worth well over a million pounds by today's standards. A Mrs Benmohel, a pillar of the community who, fortunately, kept a diary, attended Abraham in his last illness. In it she recorded how she had to provide him with many of the necessities of life, including sheets, as he slept on newspapers. She also noted down that when he was in good health he fried onions with the windows open – to give the impression that he was cooking steak, thereby putting his neighbours off the scent of his miserly habits.

There was also another contemporary Dublin Jew named Abraham Cohen, who ironically was as great a business failure as his namesake was a success. Acting as agent for a rabbit-furrier, he lent a large sum of money to a bogus prince who subsequently disappeared with it. Later, however, he achieved distinction as a first-class cook. According to Mrs Benmohel again, fried fish was his speciality, which he cooked "to a nicety, very crisp and dry". Because of this skill, and to further distinguish him from the miserly Abraham, he was known as "Fresser" Cohen – Fresser being Yiddish for someone who eats everything in sight. He died, apparently fat and contented, in 1904.

When the Irish Parliament was subsumed into the Parliament at Westminster by the Act of Union in 1801, the civil disabilities of the Jews in Ireland became identical with those in England. In 1818, the repeal of the Irish Naturalisation Act meant that Jews could now be naturalised in Ireland, but they were still barred from all civic positions and universities. Following the Catholic Emancipation Act of 1829, various attempts were made between 1833 and 1848 to pass Jews Relief Bills in Parliament, but all failed. Even Gladstone, at this stage, was against any act "whereby a Jew could be admitted to the government of a Christian country". In 1847, Baron Lionel Rothschild, elected Member of Parliament for the City of London, was not allowed to take his seat because of his refusal to swear the Christian oath. When he was returned at three subsequent elections, the same impasse occurred. Finally, in 1858, an unofficial compromise was agreed, and Rothschild took his place in the House.

Meanwhile in Dublin, the tiny number of Jews played a negligible part in public life. In the London *Sunday Times* of 18th October, 1835, the following announcement appeared:

> The Jews residing in Dublin have purchased a chapel formerly the property of a Presbyterian seceding congregation and converted it into a synagogue. This is the only one in Ireland.

While there was seating for 220 persons, the community at that time numbered only 12 families. The numbers grew slowly, and by the first Census of 1861 the total number of Jews in Ireland stood at 393, out of a total population of 5.5 million. However, by 1871 it had dropped back to 285.

In 1874, Lewis Harris, a leading member of the small community, stood as a city alderman. Having encountered religious prejudice, he wrote and delivered a letter, a plea for toleration, to every elector. He was elected with a large majority. Two years later, he died on the day that he was due to be installed as Lord Mayor of Dublin. Eighty years later, in 1956, Robert Briscoe, an early member of the IRA, would become the first Jewish Lord Mayor of Dublin.

By the early 1880s the events that would have the most crucial effect on the Jewish population of Ireland were in fact happening two thousand miles away to the east. During the two previous centuries of their settlement in the Russian Empire, Jews had learned to cope with the traditional and intermittent anti-Semitism of both Orthodox Church and autocratic government. With the accession of Alexander III in 1881, however, this random oppression became orchestrated and then systematised by the Czar and his new ministers, a collection of notorious Jew-haters. In a note to one of them, the Czar wrote: "We must never forget that it was the Jews who crucified our Lord and spilled his priceless blood." First, a series of "spontaneous pogroms" occurred throughout Southern Russia and the Ukraine. Unrestrained by the police, looting and murder were widespread. Then, in 1882, the infamous "May Laws" were introduced, effectively destroying the fabric of Jewish life throughout the Russian Empire, which by then included the Baltic States of Lithuania, Latvia, and Estonia, as well as two-thirds of Poland.

No further Jews were allowed to settle in the Pale of Settlement. Those already there were driven out of their rural communities, on the flimsiest of pretexts, and forced into the ghettoes of the larger towns. Crippling restrictions were placed on Jewish entry into high schools and universities, into the professions and most trades. Following the "May Laws" Jewish communities became isolated and pauperised.

The climax of the brutality came with the expulsion of

Jewish families living in the major cities. In Moscow, where the Czar's brother, Sergei, was Governor-General, Jews were rounded up at night. Forced to abandon all their possessions, they were manacled together and marched to the railway station. Similar scenes were repeated in St Petersburg and Kharkov. A Jewish delegation went to plead with the Czar's minister, the unspeakable and unpronounceable Pobyedonostzev, who was the architect of this policy. In turn, he explained that its intent was the death of a third of Russian Jews, the flight of another third, and the conversion of the remainder. His plan proved more successful in some aspects than others, and by the end of the century, half of Russia's four million Jews had emigrated. But very few converted, and it was left to Hitler's Nazis, fifty years later, to murder those who had stayed behind.

Inevitably, the horrors of the Holocaust now overshadow those of the pogroms. The numbers of their respective victims are not comparable, but for virtually the first half of the twentieth- century, it was the nightmare of the pogroms that haunted the Jewish imagination. And for the two million Jews of the Russian Empire who fled westward after 1882, it was the memory of the pogroms that influenced their attitudes to life around them and their relationships – usually suspicious, occasionally paranoid – with their Gentile neighbours. Of those two million emigrants, approximately a thousand arrived in Ireland – and four of them were my grandparents.

The Jews who came from Lithuania, which remained part of Russia till 1918, were known as Litvaks – as opposed to Polaks, who came from the Polish provinces of the Pale of Settlement. There was always a tremendous rivalry between Litvaks and Polaks, and each affected to despise the other. This mutual contempt was to continue long after the emigration to the West and appears largely based on the fact they pronounced their Yiddish differently – and disagreed vehemently about recipes for gefilte fish.

According to the *Encyclopedia Judaica*, the Polaks "…

associated Litvaks with the following temperament: a certain emotional dryness, the superiority of intellect over emotion, mental alertness, sharp-wittedness and pungency. Only their piety was questioned." It was predominantly Litvaks who came to Ireland. And only time would tell how the supposed characteristics of the Litvak and the Irishman would combine.

However their supposed temperament may have suited life along the Baltic, Dublin and Cork were a long way from *der heim*. Indeed it is impossible to imagine what it must have been like for a Litvak arriving in Ireland. It was, of course, then part of Britain, but few Litvaks would have known much about England, let alone Ireland. Hardly any would have spoken English. And reading English would have been more difficult, as the Russian alphabet is Cyrillic, whereas the Hebrew alphabet is normally used for Yiddish, where words are read from right to left.

There is a theory that many of the Litvaks who got off the boat in Ireland either thought it was America or were told such by unscrupulous captains or travel agents. This misconception must have occasionally happened, but it sounds more like a malicious rumour put about by Polaks to show how stupid Litvaks really were. More likely, Dublin and Cork were seen, literally and geographically, as a halfway house for America. Possibly some thought that they would work in Ireland and save enough for the rest of the fare. There are, however, few instances of Litvak Irish Jews re-emigrating to America in the first half of the 20th century. Once they had made a little money, most seemed to have settled down happily enough in Dublin, Cork, or Limerick.

There are no records to show what these immigrants thought of their host-country or its people. Yet the land they had entered shared some characteristics with the land they had left. Like Lithuania, Ireland had a predominantly Catholic peasantry, who eked out a fairly basic living on the land. Both countries had a foreign ruling class and strong nationalist movements constantly on the edge of violent rebellion; although, of the two, Ireland had the longer history of foreign oppression. And, while Ireland was known in some quarters as "the land of saints and scholars", Litvak Jews had themselves produced many scholars.

What the Irish thought of these refugees washed up on their shores is equally hard to discover, but they both had persecution and emigration in common. In the five years of the potato famine and its immediate aftermath, 1846 to 1851, over 1,000,000 people had died of starvation and disease, and 1,500,000 emigrated. As one sympathetic observer wrote in the *Cork Examiner* in 1884: "These haggard, emaciated, tattered-clothed, Jewish immigrants look not unlike our own impoverished people after the Famine."

The common pattern for most Jewish immigrants was for those with little money to become pedlars. If their peddling prospered, they noted what items sold best and set up small businesses to manufacture them, using later Jewish arrivals as their travelling salesmen – the *vekele*. Immigrants who arrived with a little capital started small shops, or if they were greater risk-takers, set up as money-lenders or pawnbrokers. In some areas, these immigrants were seen as unwelcome competition. In 1886, posters began to appear on Dublin walls urging the local citizenry to have no dealings with "these foreign Jews of recent arrival", and some pedlars were assaulted on their rounds.

Hearteningly, the Irish press hit back: "This sudden antipathy to a hard-working and inoffensive section of the population is either the product of some hare-brained set of ruffians having some ulterior motive," wrote the *Freeman's Journal*. "We may promise that the movement will enjoy a brief existence. The soil of Ireland does not take kindly to religious persecution. It has had too much bitter experience of that evil to enjoy it."

In another editorial, the *Evening Telegraph* expanded on this empathy:

The Jews have had a hard lot in the world's history. There is only one other people on the face of the earth which has suffered persecution approaching theirs, and that other people is the Irish. Ireland stands alone among nations in freedom from the odium of having persecuted the Jews, a nation sadly exiled from their own country.

Fine, high-flown sentiments, though it could be argued that, historically, there had been too few Jews in the country to test the true tolerance of the native Irish. However, for whatever reason, the posters and assaults seemingly stopped as quickly as they had started.

Meanwhile, there was the problem of providing for the growing numbers of Jews who had arrived by 1890. For example, there is a circular in the archive of the Irish Jewish Museum, dated 25th March, 1890. Issued by the core of original Anglo-Irish Jews in Dublin, and addressed "to our English co-religionists", it was basically an appeal for financial help to build a new synagogue, as the current one was "entirely unsuited". The circular goes on to give valuable insight into the makeup of the community:

> The Jews of Dublin are divided into two classes, namely: (a) the representatives of those who founded the congregation who may be said to be English or Irish Jews: (b) a large body of foreign Jews, who, for the past eight years have made Dublin their residence, and who largely outnumber the English-speaking Jews; in fact there are of the original congregation only twelve or thirteen families, while the number of foreign Jews amounts to between 600 and 700 souls ... Our foreign brethren have opened two places of worship close to each other, in the upper parts of houses, unsuitable and unhealthy. In one of the

places which we visited, we found about 200
hundred persons assembled in a room not more
than 25 feet square, and of a height not exceeding
from 8 to 9 feet.

Enough money was forthcoming to start construction of a
new synagogue in Adelaide Road, near the centre of Dublin.
More was needed to finish it. In March 1892, the expanding
community made another appeal to their fellow-citizens,
which appeared in all the main Irish newspapers. It
concluded: "The Jews of Dublin, having always contributed
to many deserving charities in the city, now ask their fellow-
citizens to reciprocate and help them in their necessity."
Editorials supported the appeal. The *Dublin Daily Express*
wrote: "We think it the bounden duty of every Christian to
assist the Jewish community in their pious work. It is our
manifest duty to help that people, who preserved for us by
their religious zeal that great book which is the foundation of
religion and virtue."

The appeal was so successful that the synagogue and
attached classrooms were completed that same year. A
handsome building, it was designed, perhaps a little incongruously, in the Eastern Romanesque style by J J O'Callaghan,
FRIAI, and built by Messrs Collen Brothers of Dublin and
Portadown for a cost of about £5,000. It was consecrated on
4th December, 1892, by the Chief Rabbi of the British Empire,
Dr Herman Adler, in front of a large and ecumenical
congregation. In his address, Dr Adler quoted from an
unnamed Irish poet: "Alas, poor Erin! thou art thyself an eternal
badge of sufferance, the blood of thy people rests not on thy
head." Dr Adler went on to urge the members of the Dublin
Hebrew Congregation to prove themselves worthy of the
hospitality and shelter extended to them in Ireland, and to
"abstain rigidly from anything that could conduce to the hurt
or harm of your fellow-citizens, and by being scrupulously fair
and honest in your dealings with them."

My own parents would be married nearly forty years later in this fine example of neo-Eastern Romanesque architecture in the heart of Dublin. By that time the Jewish community in Ireland would have grown rapidly and prospered moderately. But that all was not entirely sweetness and light earlier in the century between the Jews and the Irish was highlighted by E R Lipsett, who penned occasional pieces from Dublin for *The Jewish Chronicle* under the name Halitvak. For example, on 21st December, 1906, he wrote:

> The Irish certainly are hospitable. They are the best people on earth to visit; and to be happy you must always remain a visitor; always a guest. You must know your place and let them see that you know it. But assume for once a place as one of the family, by right of long residence and general use-fulness, then you see the other side; you see the Irish clannishness, the Irish exclusiveness. Nevertheless, there is a way of getting over these, if only you know how. Unfortunately, the Jews in Ireland have not so far succeeded in doing that. The Jews understand the Irish little; the Irish understand the Jews less. Each seems a peculiar race in the eyes of the other; and, in a word, the position of Jews in Ireland is peculiarly peculiar ... They have coined here a term which is nowhere else in circulation. Nowhere else is the term "Jewman" known, here we hear nothing else.

Having lamented the protective exclusivity of both parties, Halitvak goes on to admit that:

> Religious intolerance, so far as Jews are concerned, is practically non-existent in Ireland. All the warfare of creed is carried on between the two native sections ... Irish Protestants, it is true, are continually on the prowl for souls, but that, of course, cannot be classed as intolerance.

Catholics, however, never preach to or argue with Jews. It is to be noted too, by the way, that according to popular opinion it is easier to get along with the Catholics, and that Catholic Dublin has four times as many Jews as Protestant Belfast, though the latter is a more thriving city.

It was still early days in 1906, but by the time Ireland became a Free State, relations between the Jewish community and its neighbours had improved, in the main towns at any rate. The "peculiarly peculiar" feeling was vanishing. The next generation of Jewmen would speak with Irish accents, attend Irish schools and universities, and one of them would even play rugby for Ireland.

3. A Saturday Walk

Though three of my four Lithuanian Irish grandparents died while I was fairly young, I can still remember them – if not what their Lithuanian-Irish accents sounded like. There were the poor Prices who lived on the South Circular Road, in what used to be called Little Jerusalem, and my mother's family, the wealthy Whites, who lived in a grand house in Rathgar, in those days one of Dublin's smartest districts. I spent a lot of my childhood during the later part of World War II in what we called "the White House". I can still see the large garden, its lawns and fruit trees divided by tall privet hedges. The privet buds always fascinated me. I loved unpeeling the perfect green segments that got smaller and smaller like Russian dolls, until at the end there was nothing but emptiness, disappointment. Surely there should have been something more exciting at the heart of a privet bud. But what did I expect? An emerald? The secret of the universe written on a Fortune Cookie message?

A stone building used as a garage stood at the end of the garden. It was home to several cars, a large American model invariably amongst them. These were traded in annually. I loved the smell of their new leather and their exotic Red-Indian names – Buick, Packard, Pontiac, Chevrolet. To a five-year-old, seated in the back seat, they were huge, self-contained other worlds.

The world outside the White House made little impression on me. It was the time of de Valera's fireside chats on the radio, modelled on Roosevelt's in the US, during which Dev talked of his idyllic, pastoral ambitions for the Free State, isolated from the corrupting, industrialised materialism of the mid-20th century. Discreetly ignored were the poverty and alcoholism, the unemployment and high birth-rate that led to the continuous emigration across the Atlantic and the Irish Sea.

Totally unaware of all this, I enjoyed a near-idyllic childhood without guilt. For eight years I was an only child, and for five of those years the family's only grandchild. I was spoilt, if not by my mother, then at least by the rest of the family. I have a clear memory of sitting next to my maternal grandfather on a sofa in a large sun-lit living room. Various aunts and uncles were assembled, all listening to a big radiogram in a walnut cabinet, my Uncle Arthur's pride and joy. Neville Chamberlain was telling us that Great Britain was now at war with Nazi Germany. Everyone seemed upset, my mother particularly so. It meant she would have to stay in Dublin, while my father, now a GP in Hackney, remained in London. I however felt perfectly happy at the idea of staying on in Ireland.

The fact that we were all sitting in this grand salon in Kenilworth Square was entirely due to the energy of my grandfather, Oscar White (né Weiss). His was a rags-to-riches story. I remember him as small, rotund, highly energetic, and always dapper figure who frequently wore spats. He had arrived in Dublin around 1898. On the boat, probably boarded at Libau (Liepaja, in Russian), he fell in love with an eighteen-year-old Lithuanian-Jewish girl. His ardour was too much for her, and according to the family story, she complained to the captain, who gave her a hefty sailor as chaperone. In Dublin, Oscar Weiss became Oscar White and started to make money. To have done so, he must have had some small initial capital and been willing to take risks. Within a few years, he had progressed from money-lending into property.

That first year in Dublin he had gone to take tea at the house of an old Russian friend. There he met the young woman he had fallen in love with on the boat. Her name was Bessie Merkin. Years later I would learn that "a merkin" was a pubic wig, a popular beauty-aid in the 15th and 16th centuries – a fact that my grandmother was, mercifully, unlikely to have discovered in 19th-century Ireland. Anyway this time, on dry land, Miss Merkin was less alarmed by Oscar White's attentions, and a few months later they married. They bought a house in Victoria Street, off the South Circular Road, and proceeded to have five children, of whom my mother was the third. Within fifteen years they were all living in style in a four-storey house with privet hedges in an elegant square in Rathgar.

Oscar White died in 1939, a few months before my brother was born. It is the custom among observant Jewish families to name children after a dead blood relation, normally a grandparent. They should have the same Hebrew name, which always allows for some latitude in the English adaptation. My grandfather's Hebrew name was Asher, one of the ten lost tribes, but nobody wanted to call my brother Oscar, which was not a fashionable name at the time. Perhaps they also knew enough about its literary connections and were already anxious that he should grow up to be a heterosexual doctor. In any event, my mother had just seen *Gone with the Wind* and fallen for Leslie Howard, who played the elegant Southern gentleman Ashley Wilkes. Which is how the more plebian Stanley, named after a great-grandfather called Solomon (Schlomo in Hebrew), ended up with a brother called Ashley.

While I loved the lower floors of the White House in Kenilworth Square, I was terrified of the top floor, where I slept. When I went to bed I felt isolated, miles away from the grown-ups several floors below. And if I wanted to pee in the night, I had to creep out of my bedroom and go up another half-floor to the toilet. That was how I encountered my first insomniac – Grandma White. At the time she seemed a rather remote old lady. She wore glasses that seemed to magnify her

SOMEWHERE TO HANG MY HAT

"The White House" (57 Kenilworth Square, Rathgar) as it looks today. There used to be silvered stone lions at the bottom of the steps.

watery eyes – she would eventually go blind – and I found her language hard to understand. When I was older I realised it had been Irish-English sprinkled with genuine Russian as well as Litvak-Yiddish.

En route to that terrifying eyrie of a toilet, I would pass her half-open bedroom door, where I could hear mumbling. One night, on the way back, she called out to me, and I went in. She was sitting up in bed, reading. She said that she read most nights when she couldn't sleep, nearly always the same book – *War and Peace* in Russian. Moreover she read it aloud because she liked the sound of the language and didn't want to forget it. The mumbling I had heard was Russian mumbling. This meeting must have taken place after her husband had died, as she was in the bedroom alone, Oscar White having died of a heart attack when he was only fifty-seven.

Later, when I asked her what else she read, she replied, *Anna Karenina* – also in Russian. And when she had it finished, she went back to *War and Peace*. If you are only going to read two books, I suppose those are not a bad choice. She must have assumed it was impossible to obtain other books in

Russian in Dublin. Still, I wondered why she only brought two Tolstoy novels with her? Had she left her home in Skud in a hurry and just grabbed those two? Was her luggage limited, and those two her favourites? And which one was she reading on the boat when her future husband had pestered her? There are so many questions left to ask, yet no one left to answer them.

For most of those War years I lived, with my mother and brother, in the White House in Kenilworth Square. I was never bored exploring the rooms or gardens, back and front. There were numerous living and reception rooms. Some which were not in daily use had paintings in ornate frames and elaborate display cabinets containing bric-à-brac, mostly miniatures. Grandpa White was a great collector, and his collection eventually sold for a very large sum. The best paintings were kept in a large study where all the men of the household were expected to say their morning prayers. First thing in the morning this gathering created another loud mumble, only a Hebrew, not a Russian, mumble. One morning, a new maid – the housekeeper stayed but the maids changed frequently – came running down the stairs in hysterics. She couldn't dust in the big study because there was a swarm of bees in there. She was terrified of bees. My grandmother told her she was safe enough with praying Jews.

The good fortune that blessed the White family had not touched the Prices. They lived only two miles away, but a whole world apart. My main memory of visiting them was whenever my father managed to come over to Dublin for a long weekend, or for one of the religious holidays. On those occasions the visits to the Prices became a Saturday afternoon ritual. We had to walk there, as my father wouldn't drive on the Sabbath, except on an urgent medical call. Once there, we had tea with them, because my mother refused to eat any other meal with them on account of their cooking. Later I would associate that Saturday walk, like his reception of his sisters' letters, with my father's feelings of guilt. He was clearly uneasy about staying with his rich in-laws and the fact that my childhood, unlike his, had become a spoilt and privileged one. I once overheard the end of an argument between my parents: my mother angrily telling him that if he wanted to go and stay there he could – but we would stay here. Anyway they hadn't got room for us. That Saturday she didn't come visiting with us.

Normally we started off our Sabbath pilgrimage around a quarter to three. I say "around" because there was another ritual played out just prior to departure. My mother's given name, a closely kept secret, because she disliked it so much, was Gertrude, but everyone called her Gypsy for obvious reasons. Very dark and striking-looking, she loved brightly coloured clothes, hats, beads, and bracelets. Indeed she never quite grew out of her Twenties' flapper image. As my father waited impatiently in the hall, my mother, in full rig, would come down the stairs. Oedipally unaware at the time, I thought she looked lovely. My father, however, looked distinctly uncomfortable. I came to know that look well in various situations. It meant my mother was drawing attention to herself, and my father was embarrassed. She knew that look too.

"What's wrong?" she would say defensively.

He was no good at criticism or confrontation – except in anger.

"Haven't you got something else?"

"No," she said. "What's wrong with it?"

"It's all too ..." he said, making sweeping motions with his hands, taking in everything from the colour of her blouse, the necklaces and bangles, to the elegant high heels.

"Do you want me to go there wearing old clothes? Like a rag-woman?"

He always went white, not red, with anger.

"Please, Gyp." He tried discreetly to indicate my attentive presence.

He had just come from ministering to the sick of Hackney

and the casualties of the Blitz at all hours of the day and night. He was only here for a few days. My mother turned round and went back upstairs. Some minutes later she reappeared in a darker blouse, a few ornaments less, and flatter heels. She was not exactly a rag-woman, but she had done enough to mollify my father. We set out – around quarter to three.

The front door of the White House was on the first floor. One came down broad steps, at the bottom of which were two silvered stone lions, couchant, then down the front path and out into Kenilworth Square. I was like the King leaving his Versailles, going out to see his people – on the South Circular Road. We walked round two sides of the square, which was totally surrounded by a huge privet hedge. I was never able to see inside the square, but I could hear the soft plunk of tennis balls. My mother was a fine tennis player, but she had never played there. It was a club that didn't admit Jews. It was the first example of overt anti-Semitism that I had ever heard. To combat such exclusions, Dublin Jews started the Carlisle Tennis and Cricket Club. My mother won the club tournament two years running, wearing a long white bandeau in imitation of the then Wimbledon champion, Suzanne Lenglen. It helped fuel the Gypsy image. Her brother Michael was one of the men's top players. A display case in the best reception room of the White House was full of the cups and medals they had won for tennis and swimming. The Whites prided themselves on being good at sport. Ashley and I were to learn that no less was expected of us.

As we turned onto the Harold's Cross Road, the rich, detached houses of tranquil Rathgar were already left behind. Here was traffic and rows of smaller, Victorian terraces. There were different smells too. I always imagined one was of fried bacon – a taboo food, a taboo smell, so how I imagined the smell I have no idea. We then walked past the long, high, stone walls of the Convent of St Clare. The big wooden gates were always closed, yet I longed to know what they did inside. There was no chink anywhere to peep through. I never saw a nun, or anybody else, go in or out. Whatever went on within remained a mystery.

That Convent came to symbolise the great divide. Everything beyond it, shops, houses, even people, seemed to become visibly smaller and poorer. The smells became more pungent, the bacon mixed in with something even stronger, and I would realise with increasing gloom that we were in the land of my grandparents Price. It wasn't their fault that the Grand Canal ran just behind their house. Horse-drawn barges still went up and down it. When an east wind blew, the smell of dung mixed in with the strong whiffs of malt from the Guinness Brewery at St James's Gate. We turned left just before we reached Clanbrassil Street, which for the first half of the century was the commercial centre of Jewish life in Dublin. It was here, according to my father, that James Joyce had found the model for Leopold Bloom, a man my father knew, who had a half-share in a chemist shop.

As we walked along the south bank of the Canal, all manner of garbage floated by. We next crossed over Sally's Bridge onto the South Circular Road, where my grandparents lived with their three unmarried daughters, all by then in their thirties. The middle daughter, Hilda, was the same age as my mother. If I hated the smell in the open air of the South Circular Road, it was even more noxious to me inside my grandparents' house. Small and ill-ventilated, it seemed impregnated with a particular smell. The family rarely ate meat, more out of economy than choice. Their big treat was plaice, boiled in milk, with slices of onion. Whether this was a Litvak-Jewish or just a plain Baltic custom didn't interest me. I loathed boiled milk and the smell of it makes me retch to this day. As for the foul, wrinkled skin that forms on it, I find it hard to write the words – let alone be in the same house with it.

The tragedies that happened in that household multiplied as I grew older, but my earliest memories are of embarrassment and the dawning of social guilt. I knew it was wrong to have a sinking heart as I went from the rich to the poor side of town. I knew it was wrong to dread that walk with my father on his brief visits to Dublin. Wrong to want to stay behind the secure, silver railings of Kenilworth Square and not be dragged out into the smell of horse-shit and boiled milk on the South Circular Road. Wrong I knew, but that was the way I felt. At the age of eight, I was already a "Champagne socialist".

When we arrived, everyone there made a great fuss of me. They wanted to spoil me with cake and chocolate, despite my father's objections. On my best behaviour, I let them pinch my cheek, say how I'd grown, and patiently answered all their questions about what I did at school. My paternal grandfather made me read something from the prayer book, which I dutifully did, after which he slipped me a silver coin, a harp on one side, and a horse on the other. It was the first Irish money I was to earn, and I got it for reading Hebrew.

My paternal grandmother, Sarah, was a kindly lady from an academic and musical family, the Shreiders of Shmergon. She endured considerable ill health, and spent a lot of time in bed with a combination of diabetes, high blood pressure, and a bad back. Of the five children, two boys and three girls, my father was the only one to marry. Marks, the eldest, also became a doctor and was an officer in the Royal Flying Corps during the Great War. Afterwards he bought a surgery and practiced in North London. He always drove a new Riley, black with a long bonnet. In London he took me for drives, plying me with Fox's Glacier Mints, which he kept in the glove compartment. Later, I realised he sucked them to sweeten his breath, as he was a heavy pipe-smoker. With his curved pipe in his mouth, he bore a strong physical resemblance to Sherlock Holmes. He never ate meat, and whenever he came to eat with us in London he brought his own kippers, which he handed over to my mother to cook for him. Marks was six years older than my father and very close to him.

Minnie, Hilda, and Polly were the three sisters, their story already Irish-Jewish Chekhov, though at the time my theatrical experience was limited to the annual Pantomime at the Gaiety. In any event our visits must have been fraught with tension for everyone. The three sisters were smiling and hospitable to their clever brother who'd escaped to join his other brother across the water. Two sons, two doctors, the greatest pride and joy any Jewish family can have. To cap it, brother Jim – whom no one ever called by his real name, Morris – had married one of the richest and best-looking girls in Dublin. They had produced a son too, a seemingly polite and clever boy, who let you pinch his cheeks and pat his head, but never seemed to eat much lunch.

They may have been proud of us, waiting for our visits. Or they may have hated our polite, patronising calls. Either way, as the plot on the South Circular Road developed, it would eventually move out of Chekhov into Tennessee Williams territory. It was to be a long-running drama, and my original walk-on part would grow and grow. However, the one character I have omitted from the scene was the most important of all – the man of the house, small, with a reddish beard, in a brown suit with waistcoat, standing there praying in the right-hand corner, my grandfather – Charles Beresford Price.

4. In Search of Charles Beresford Price

As far as anyone knew, the name of my paternal grandfather since he arrived in Ireland had always been Charles Beresford Price. He had no relations anywhere else in Ireland of that, or any other, name. Born in Tels, Lithuania, a great centre of Jewish learning, and renowned for its *yeshivah*, (a talmudic college) he had apparently left with his two brothers after the pogroms of the early 1880s and sailed for America. The family story was that he had been seasick all the way as far as Ireland, where the boat had docked. Telling his brothers that he could go no farther, that

Charles Beresford Price.

he would never go on a boat again, he unilaterally disembarked. The two brothers went on to America, settled down, and multiplied. I can testify to the multiplying.

In 1975, I was working briefly in Los Angeles – briefly, I discovered, being the best way to work there. A stage play had been optioned by an American film-producer. Unusually and gratifyingly, he had asked the playwright himself to write the screenplay. The play was set in England, and he wanted me to Americanise it. This task didn't present a problem, as I had worked as a journalist for four years in New York and had become bi-lingual. However, the screenplay itself was destined to join the thousands of commissioned scripts that don't get made every year. Still, I was enjoying the pool, the tennis, the avocado dip, when early in my stay someone named Fred Price called me. Or rather I called him. My agent wouldn't give him my number in case he was a mad, homicidal Price. In Los Angeles you can't be too careful.

Fred Price sounded perfectly sane. A studio carpenter at MGM, he had seen my name in a column of *The Hollywood Reporter*, that snapper-up of unconsidered trifles, announcing the arrival in town of an English writer called Stanley Price.

"Do you have an Irish grandfather?" he asked.

"Yes, but how do you know?"

Fred Price knew about it through his family. He had an uncle in Chicago who had conducted an occasional correspondence over the years with my father who was a remote cousin. My father must have told him about his son the writer. Fred Price then invited me over to North Hollywood, to meet him, his wife and kids, and have dinner. I have never had any luck on blind dates, but it would have seemed churlish not to accept. I insisted that his wife shouldn't go to any trouble. I was working hard, I said, and would only come for a drink.

"Fine, fine," he said. "Anything you like. So just come by for a drink." We made an arrangement for Sunday week.

On the day I studied the map, listed down all the vital

freeway exit numbers, sellotaped them to my windscreen, negotiated the spaghetti junctions, and eventually found my way to North Hollywood. Fred Price lived in a cul-de-sac of modest clapboard houses. Inevitably there were numerous cars, and parking wasn't easy. I rang the bell. The door was opened by a friendly looking man, maybe ten years older than me, and dressed in Western style. "You Stanley," he said, "me Fred," greeting me like a long-lost brother. Behind him the house was packed out.

"Is this some sort of convention?" I asked.

"Sure," he said. "A Price Convention. Joint is knee-deep in Prices."

There were Prices by blood, by marriage, by remarriage, by adoption, from California, from out-of-state, Prices of all shapes and sizes. It was Price cars that jammed up the street. This encounter was no ordinary blind date, it was the mother and father, the *zeyde* and *buba* of all blind dates: Meanwhile every Price in the place stampeded to meet their Anglo-Irish cousin. After ten minutes I was exhausted. Suddenly we were all summoned into the garden to eat.

"But you said just a drink," I gasped at my host.

"You said just a drink," Fred beamed at me, "but if you don't want to eat, don't eat."

What followed would, in any other country, be called a three-day banquet. Here it was merely a barbecue. The hospitality and goodwill were overwhelming. Everybody inevitably loved my accent. An outsider, looking at that motley gathering, could never have guessed that the only thing we had in common was a surname. Fred came up and put his arm round me, "How about this, hey? Even the gatecrashers here are called Price!"

In the end it was the name that proved the problem.

"How did we get it?" they asked, and looked to me for the answer.

"I don't know," I said lamely.

"But where does the name come from?"

"Lithuania."

"No, you don't understand. We've all have had this name since our family came to America. What was it before we came to America?"

I admitted further ignorance. Their faces fell. I tried an informed guess.

"Maybe there's some word like it in Lithuanian or Russian."

I could see that didn't satisfy them. But by now, after just a few drinks and a lot of barbecue, I was feeling very attached to my new family. If only I could have answered their questions. However the Fred Price International Reunion did inspire me to go out into the world and find an answer.

A year later, another play of mine took me to Tel Aviv, where I went to the Museum of the Diaspora, a fascinating place devoted to the history of Jewish communities round the world. In the main hall were magnificent models of historic synagogues, including one of the Great Synagogue of Vilna, which I had heard my Grandma White talk about. I worked out that she must have been in it in the early 1880s. Beyond the exhibits was a computer room where you could type in your name, or the place where your family came from, and get a printout of relevant information. I tapped P-R-I-C-E into the computer. After a moment the screen flashed up a list of names beginning with PR in various languages. The nearest to mine was P-R-E-U-S-S – which was German for "Prussian".

I didn't like that for a start. It conjured up a genealogical line of large, militaristic Junkers with bullet-heads, their collars too tight for their shaved stiff-necks. The only good thing about Bismark, I'd always felt, was the herring named after him. Had he not united Germany, two world wars might have been avoided. Then suddenly I realised my dates were out. My ancestral Preusses would have left Prussia well before the locals started shaving their necks and strutting about.

Back home I consulted Martin Gilbert's *Jewish History Atlas,* which showed Jewish migration patterns since medieval times. Marked by thick black arrows, the migrations were as complicated as those Los Angeles freeways. The oppressions, pogroms, and straightforward massacres had been ubiquitous, and the flights to safety ran in all directions. After suffering the atrocities of the Crusaders en route to the Holy Land – a kind of dress rehearsal on the Jews before the massacre of the Muslims – the depleted Jewish communities of the Rhineland moved steadily northwards and eastwards. In the 13th century King Boleslav the Pious welcomed Jews into Poland, and his successors, Casimir the Great and Sigismund I, gave them protective and advantageous charters. Meanwhile other migrations stretched into North Germany and the states that became Prussia. Eventually these peoples pushed eastwards along the Baltic coast into Lithuania, an unhappy country that constantly changed hands between Poland and Russia. Indeed there is a Litvak story of the old Jew who comes home to his wife and tells her that a treaty has just been signed and now they are part of Poland. "Thank God," she says, "no more of those freezing Russian winters."

After 1835, most of what had been Lithuania was absorbed into the Pale of Settlement, the series of Jewish ghettos scattered along the western side of the Russian Empire. In many of these communities people were often given the name of the last place they had come from. It seemed a valid guess that my family had moved along the Baltic from Prussia into Lithuania, possibly in search of ever-better herrings to pickle. There they had been called Preuss, and the name stuck. Now, consider this – you arrive in Ireland, you are asked your name, and you say "Preuss". The immigration officer only has to repeat it with an Irish accent – "Price, is it? Ah, Mr Price, céad míle fáilte." I suspected some of the immigration officers at Ellis Island might have been Irish too, but even if they weren't, Preuss sounds awfully like Price in most English accents. Satisfied, I sent the results of my researches to Fred Price in Los Angeles. He could circularise the other Preusses.

So much for the transatlantic Prices, but for us Anglo-Irish Prices only half of the mystery was solved. Preuss becomes Price, but what about the Charles Beresford? How was a small, very orthodox, red-bearded, Lithuanian Jew given such a grand Establishment name? None of the surviving members of the family had any idea. He had been Charles Beresford Price since his first sighting in Dublin. Searching through the family papers still kept by Aunts Minnie and Hilda didn't turn up any official documents of any kind.

Tracking down the origins of my grandfather's name was not a major priority in my life at the time, and I let the trail go cold. Some years later I was glancing at a book on naval history, and there on the page in front of me was his name, Charles Beresford. Except it was Admiral Lord Charles Beresford, hero of Alexandria. A wild coincidence maybe, but I still looked him up in an old *Dictionary of National Biography*. His entry reads:

> *BERESFORD, Charles William de la Poer, 1st Baron (1846 - 1919). Irish-born naval commander, born in Philipstown, Offaly, son of the fourth Marquis of Waterford. He entered the navy in 1859, and was promoted captain in 1882 for his services at the bombardment of Alexandria. He was a lord of the Admiralty (1886 - 88), but resigned, and sat in Parliament as Conservative member for Waterford. He later commanded the Mediterranean Fleet (1905-07), and the Channel Fleet (1907 - 09). A trenchant naval critic, he clashed with Admiral Lord Fisher over naval policy and reforms.*

Waterford – that was the clue. Our own Charles Beresford and his brothers had sailed from the Baltic for America. It struck me their route wouldn't have taken them via Dublin, but via Queenstown, now Cobh, the port of Cork, from where the Titanic and the Lusitania had both made their last sailings. This port was where my grandfather would have landed. Cork was only seventy miles from Waterford, and the Marquises of

Waterford were big landowners in the area. Also, Lord Charles had been a local MP around the time my grandfather arrived. Further research showed that, apart from being a naval hero and an MP, he was a close friend of the Prince of Wales and had a reputation as a playboy. Everybody would have known of him. My grandfather, patriotically green from seasickness all the way from Lithuania, would have gone into Immigration as a Preuss and come out as a Price. For good measure, they must have tagged on the Charles Beresford – "With a name like that, won't yer man have a grand start in his new country!" The fact that yer man didn't speak a word of English or Gaelic must have made it even funnier. More poignant was the irony of a poor, seasick Litvak being named after an Anglo-Irish naval hero.

To put my theories to the test, I had to trace the immigration records. As Ireland was still part of Britain when he landed, he would have been dealt with by the British immigration authorities, even though the port would have been manned by local staff. I contacted the Public Records Office at Kew, who hold records of immigration for England, Scotland, and Wales, only to learn that when the British left Ireland in 1922, they had left all their records behind. Thus I would have to search over there. Combining a holiday with a growing obsession, I borrowed a friend's house near Cork and began my inquiries.

The trail soon led to Gerald Goldberg, a tall, imposing-looking man, with an extraordinarily alert mind and memory for an 86 year-old. He had been a solicitor, a Lord Mayor of Cork, and was an expert on the Jewish communities of Cork and Limerick. He spoke Gaelic, Hebrew, and Yiddish, had a fine library, and was an expert on Joyce. His father had come from Akmeyan, also in Lithuania, and had originally settled in Limerick.

"Is that the Akmeyan near Trissik?" I asked.

He looked startled. "Trissik was a little village down the road. How do you know that?"

The name had struck a chord in my memory, not touched for at least thirty years. I explained how my maternal grandmother, Grandma White, when she wanted to dismiss people as nobodies from the back of beyond, used to say "Ah, they're from Akmeyan and Trissak."

"And where was she from?" Gerald Goldberg asked.

"Skud," I said.

"And that was so central?" he said. "Maybe three more people lived there than in Akmeyan!"

It seemed many of the immigrants to Cork and Limerick were Akmeyaners. As it was, his own father had left Limerick for Cork after an altercation with the small synagogue there. Gerald Goldberg lamented the disputatiousness of orthodox Jews. Even in the smallest communities, there were inevitable arguments about the finer points of social and religious practice. Splinter groups formed from the tiniest synagogues. For my part, I reminded him that Calvin and Luther weren't Jewish.

In Cork, Goldberg's father had realised there was an opportunity for a shochat, a ritual slaughterer, so he walked to Dublin, some 150 miles, where he knew he could learn the trade. He came back to Cork a fully qualified kosher butcher. His son, Gerald, recalled a conversation he had had with one of the last of the original community's surviving members. The man remembered arriving in Cork with a small boatload of fellow-Jews. On their first evening they lodged in a street round the corner from a Catholic seminary. When the news spread that some Jews had arrived, there was immediate curiosity. Clearly no Corkonian had ever seen a Jew before. A good-humoured crowd gathered and clamoured for a look at the new arrivals. Not supprisingly given recent experience, the Jews thought their last hour had come. Barring all the doors and windows, they started saying their final prayers. Fortunately, a priest from the seminary passed by and, realising what was happening, dispersed the crowd.

Gerald Goldberg talked sadly about the present-day Cork Community. From its heyday of a hundred or so families in the 1920s and 1930s, it has now dropped to a mere handful, not even enough to form a *minyan* in the unused, locked-up synagogue. To find the necessary ten male adults for a service at the New Year and Day of Atonement, they had to import a half-dozen young males from Dublin and put them up in a hotel.

Gerald Goldberg produced the earliest records of the Cork synagogue. There was no mention of a Charles Beresford Price. Yet a Jew as orthodox as my grandfather would have belonged to a synagogue. If he had been in Cork, he couldn't have been there for long. I put my theory of how he had come by the Charles Beresford. Gerald Goldberg was amused, but dubious. He didn't believe the immigration officers handed out new names, rather they usually went for the nearest English equivalent. He pointed to the list of first names of the early Cork congregants, a host of Abrahams, Isaacs, Jacobs, Hyams, and Eleazars. He asked if I remembered my grandfather's name in Hebrew. Miraculously, it came back to me. At my father's funeral, his Hebrew name was used – Moishe ben Bezalel Dov. Morris, son of Bezalel Dov. "Doesn't sound much like Charles Beresford, does it?" I said. Gerald thought Bezalel was a name from the Bible, but it scarcely suggested Beresford, let alone Charles. I asked him then about immigration records, but he had never seen any. He had once traced an uncle's original name, for the purpose of getting a passport, through his naturalisation papers at the Public Records Office at Kew. However, I didn't believe my grandfather had ever been naturalised. And as he had never left Ireland again, he hadn't needed a passport.

Much as I liked Cork, the trail for Charles Beresford there was over. Drawing a series of blanks with official sources in Cork and Cobh, I discovered that any immigration records from that period would be held in Dublin. It was time for the National Archive. However, in Dublin, I went first to the Jewish cemetery in Dolphin's Barn, a stone's throw from the

Price house on the South Circular Road. It is not an over-populated graveyard, and the tombstone was easy to find – Section B, Row 7, Plot 14. The inscription was simple: *Charles B Price. Died 27th August, 1940. Deeply mourned by his beloved wife, Sarah, sons, Marks and Morris, and daughters, Polly, Minnie and Hilda. The memory of the righteous shall be for a blessing.* There was no date or place of birth, no original name in Hebrew. No solution there, but standing in front of his grave, I worked out when he would have got married. My father was born in 1897. His brother, Marks, the eldest in the family, was six years older, thus born in 1891. As was the custom, their parents were probably married nine months or so before. There must be a marriage certificate registered sometime in 1890. He would only have been in Ireland a few years by then, and maybe he was married under his original name.

The Registry of Births, Marriages and Deaths in Dublin 2 was almost entirely full of anxious North Americans trying to trace their ancestry. The staff scurried backwards and forwards delivering big, leather-bound registers to these avid visitors and making photocopies as the relevant entries were found. This entire emotional maelstrom was constantly punctuated by cries of delight when the seekers found what they were looking for, often followed by sobbing and weeping now that they had secured a lineage going back to a Connemara peasant, who had likely been starved into emigration by an unfeeling British government. I felt the IRA would have done well there, collecting subscriptions.

My guess had been correct, and I found my grandfather's marriage certificate without too much difficulty. It told me that on the "26th March, 1890, Charles Beresford Price, bachelor, age - full, profession - pedlar, son of Mordecai Price (deceased), farmer, had married Sarah Shreider, spinster, age - full, daughter of Matthew Shreider, teacher". No clue there. I had a sneaking feeling the origins of my grandfather's name lay outside the realm of historical proof. While I was there I also found my father's birth certificate for the 7th August, 1897. His father was registered as Charles Beresford Price, but by then his professional status had improved to "Draper".

I next went to the National Archive, a solemn and impressive place, unconducive to noisy sobbing. A helpful curator told me that nearly all historic records, including early immigration files, had been housed in the Records Office, attached to the Four Courts, which had been destroyed by fire. Designed by the Regency architect James Gandon, this beautiful building had been seized by the Anti-Treaty forces in 1922 and bombarded by Michael Collins's new Free State Army. Some years later, when I saw this scene graphically re-enacted in the film Michael Collins, I could scarcely stay in my seat. When Liam Neeson, as Collins, gave the order to the artillery to fire, I wanted to shout "No, no! For God's sake, don't. My Grandfather's real name is in there!" The Four Courts was finely restored, but nothing was done about my grandfather's records.

The curator suggested that I try the records from the Chief Secretary's Office in Dublin Castle, which were also now housed in the Archive. She led me to shelves full of large red leather ledgers. I would have to look up the relevant years under each subject heading – Immigration, Jews, Russia, Lithuania. I found nothing under any of these headings between 1882 and 1900, except an entry in 1886 which read "JEWS, inflammatory placards as to". As I was about to abandon my search, the curator returned with a blue folder. It was dated 1902-3 but not listed in the registers. She said it was all she could find from the Chief Secretary's files pertaining specifically to Jews. The nearest item it contained with any relevance to immigration were comparative figures for Jews in Ireland from the censuses of 1891 and 1901.

This increasing number of Jews, and their activities, was clearly causing some concern to the British Government's Chief Secretary. On the 2nd February, 1903, he wrote a confidential letter from Dublin Castle to the Inspector

	1891 Census	1901 Census
Dublin	971	2048
Cork	62	359
Limerick	93	171
Total	1779	3898

Comparative figures for Jews in Ireland from the censuses of 1891 and 1901.

General of the Royal Irish Constabulary:

> In continuation of our conversation of this date I beg to bring to your notice that it has been stated to me that Jews in certain localities are getting the peasantry into debt. It has also been stated that Jews are in the habit of collecting from hotels, and other large establishments of the sort, used tea leaves, drying them, mixing them with deleterious drugs, and selling the compound to the poorer classes as tea; and it has been suggested that this product must be injurious to health, even producing nervous disease and insanity. Will you kindly ascertain whether there is any foundation in fact for these reports.

This extraordinary letter is signed by the Chief Secretary, the Right Honourable George Wyndham, MP.

It is worth considering this moment in Imperial history. Dublin was the second city of the greatest empire the world had ever known, the Boer War had just ended, Balfour had become Prime Minister, a speed limit of 20 mph had been introduced, George Bernard Shaw's *Man and Superman* had premièred, and in Dublin Castle the Chief Secretary for Ireland was giving official credence to a form of blood libel against the Jews, only this time tea instead of blood. In a heavily tea-drinking country like Ireland, this charge would of course have been a very appropriate twist. His fears conjure up an interesting twin-pronged conspiracy theory. Whilst the tea-drinking masses sank through "nervous disease" into "insanity", diabolic Jewish money-lenders would be busy repossessing Irish farms. The Anglo-Irish land-owning class would eventually be replaced by a Jewish one, and the debilitated and/or insane Irish peasantry replaced by an Eastern European Jewish one. And a further corollary – the Zionists would no longer need Palestine, as Ireland would already have become their Promised Land. In the long term this development might have meant no Middle East crisis. Rather two major international crises would have been merged into one, as the Jews struggled to regain Ulster for a united Jewish Ireland.

The details of what actually transpired were also contained in that blue file. After this request from the Castle, the Inspector General of the RIC had no alternative but to circulate the Chief Constables of all thirty-two counties to provide answers to the two questions. The thirty-two sets of answers were also in the file. Some Chief Constables had easier tasks than others. One simply replied "There are no Jews in Mayo". The Chief Constable in Cork replied "There are no Jew tea-dealers in Cork, and no instance has come under notice of Jews collecting tea-leaves at hotels for the purpose stated". The Detectives' Office of the Dublin Constabulary found no Jewish proceedings against any Irishman for debt and no sign of Jews scavenging in hotel dustbins for old tea-leaves. They did, however, include a couple of interesting statistics. Of the 2,000-odd Jews in Dublin, 170 had pedlars' licences, and there were 47 registered money-lenders. The Chief Constable of Limerick, somewhat keener, reported "I have found two cases of farmers in debt to Jew money-lenders, but one case has already been settled. As regards the other matter, I have been into several of their homes, and taken away samples of their tea. It is now with the public analyst."

In the following year, 1904, Limerick had the dubious

distinction of hosting Ireland's only pogrom. A tiny one, as pogroms go, it was fomented by the preaching of a Redemptorist priest, Father Creagh. His sermons were a mixture much as before, only with an Irish accent. He vilified the Jews for their methods of business, for crucifying the Lord, and, if allowed, he ranted, they would "kidnap and slay Christian children for their blood". A boycott of all Jewish businesses resulted from Creagh's crusade, as well as actual assaults on the local rabbi and other members of the community. Fortunately, there were no serious injuries, and the Irish press reacted in the same vein as they had against the Dublin posters in 1886. The Editor of *The Daily Express* wrote:

> I am sure many of you will want to join with me in condemning the utterances of one, who by education and Christian teaching, should know better than to publicly preach against a race of people who, as every Irishman knows, are good citizens, hospitable neighbours, and staunch and true friends. I feel ashamed of my religion today (the only time I have done so) when I think the exponent of such views could be a teacher of Catholicity.

Michael Davitt, the great patriot and founder of the Land League, was even more impassioned in the *Freeman's Journal*:

> There is not an atom of truth in the horrible allegations of ritual murder against this persecuted race ... I protest, as an Irishman and a Christian, against this spirit of barbarous malignity being introduced into Ireland ... Like our own race, the Jews have endured persecutions, the records of which will for ever remain a reproach to the "Christian" nations of Europe.

However, Arthur Griffith, editor of *The United Irishman*, used the outcry over Father Creagh for his own purposes:

Twenty years ago we had few Jews in Ireland. Today
we have Jewish magistrates to teach us respect for
the glorious constitution under which we exist;
Jewish lawyers to look after our affairs; and Jewish
money-lenders to accomodate us; Jewish tailors to
clothe us; Jewish photographers to take our
pictures; Jewish brokers to furnish our houses; and
Jewish auctioneers to sell us up·in the end for the
benefit of all our other Jewish benefactors.

The sarcasm is a touch heavy, the exaggeration palpably
ludicrous. No Irishman really believed that in 1904 the country
was full of Jewish magistrates and lawyers, let alone
photographers and auctioneers. Money-lenders and tailors
maybe. But Griffith was a rare bird in the Irish aviary, a believer
in the International Jewish conspiracy. Obsessed with the
Dreyfus Case in France, he penned endless editorials about it to
prove that the Jews had undermined the fabric of every country
in which they lived, such as in 1899 when he wrote:

The Jew has at heart no country but the Promised
Land. He forms a nation apart wherever he goes. He
may be a German citizen today, and a British subject
tomorrow. He is always a Jew nationalist bound by
the most solemn obligations and the fiercest hopes
to the achievement of National Restoration and
Revenge. Touch a Jew in Warsaw, and collections
will be made to protect him in Moorish synagogues
on the edge of the Sahara and in Chinese synagogues
on the Yellow River. The French Army has sent a Jew
to a convict settlement. So, woe to the French Army
if the Jews can manage it.

Cleverly hedging his bets, Griffith's could claim that
Dreyfus's release and reinstatement was, as forecast, another
coup for the Jewish conspiracy. Griffith subsequently founded
Sinn Fein, the party and its newspaper, led the delegation with
Michael Collins that negotiated the Treaty with Lloyd George,

and, in 1922, became first President of the Dáil. Six months later he died of a massive stroke, broken in health and heart, it was said, by the Civil War. His ludicrous anti-Semitism was never mentioned after he became a hero of the Free State.

The last word on the Limerick pogrom, however, must lie with Marcus Joseph Blond, a small Jewish businessman, who had a letter in *The Times* on the 10th April 1904:

> It took me all these years, with the greatest pain and trouble and working unceasingly until I established myself comfortably and enjoyed a nice trade, until, all of a sudden, like a thunderstorm, hatred and animosity were preached against the Jews, how they crucified the Lord Jesus, how they martyred St Simon, and gradually in one month's time, I have none of my previous customers coming into my shop. In fact, my business is nil at the present. Would you call my trade a national evil? I defy anyone in this city to say whom I have wronged. What did I overcharge? Since the beginning of the crusade of Father Creagh against the Jews we never got a fair chance to defend ourselves or put our case rightly before the public.

The boycott petered out, the Church disowned Father Creagh, and he was withdrawn from Limerick. However, the damage had been done, and the Jewish population there dwindled. It revived a little around World War II, but at present Limerick is down to its last Jew.

The fact that distinguished Irishmen, with few exceptions, spoke out when their words were needed, and wrote strongly in the press against anti-Semitism, gave the virus little serious hold in Irish life, even though it is in the nature of a virus to linger. Despite Griffith's death in 1922, pockets of anti-Semitism remained in the Church and various establishment institutions. There was always to be some suspicion of the foreigner, and for another generation "the Jewman" was still predominantly regarded as an outsider.

In his essay "What It Means to Be a Jew", published in 1942 in *The Bell* magazine, A J Leventhal, a professor of English Literature at Trinity and close friend of Samuel Beckett, recalls the encounters of his youth between Jewish and Catholic street gangs on Lombard Street West, the border between Little Jerusalem and its equally impoverished non-Jewish neighbours. These confrontations were scarcely of *West Side Story* dimensions, and they consisted mainly of the Catholic gang chanting in mock-Hebraic accents:

Two shilling, two shilling, the Jewman did cry.
For a fine pair of blankets from me you did buy.
Do you think me vun idgeet or vun bloomin fool?
If I dont get my shillin I must have my vool.

According to Leventhal, the young Jewmen retorted:

Two pennies, two pennies the Christians did shout,
For a bottle of porter or Guinnesss stout.
My wifes got no shawl and my kids have no shoes
But I must have my money, I must have my booze.

Apart from sounding well-rehearsed, the chants neatly reflected early mutual prejudices – the avaricious Jewish pedlar versus the feckless Irish boozer. Leventhal goes on to shed light on the unique use of the expression "Jewman" in Ireland, which he claims derives from the constant use of the Gaelic fir, "a man", which attached to most national descriptions as in "the Italian-man", "the Russia-man". It originally carried no pejorative meaning and was first used in print in J M Synge's *Playboy of the Western World* where Pegeen Mike declares "And myself, a girl, was tempted often to go sailing the seas till I'd marry a Jewman with ten kegs of gold."

In any event, I emerged from the National Archive no nearer solving the mystery of Charles Beresford Price. Furthermore, I had to consider that rather than immigration officers giving him the name, he might have adopted it himself. If the real Charles Beresford were well-known in Ireland, my grandfather might have also heard of him and thought it a grand and impressive name for his new life as an Irish pedlar. Such an explanation seemed unlikely, though, for someone who had arrived in Ireland speaking only Russian and Yiddish. Given their respective Cyrillic and Hebrew alphabets, he couldn't have interpreted a newspaper headline, let alone understood a news story. And it seems equally improbable that he could have learned enough English between his post-1882 landing and his 1890 marriage, never mind understood enough of English social distinctions, to have adopted that aristocratic name for his marriage certificate. Had he been that smart, that far-sighted, that socially-aspirant in such an alien culture, he should have ended up living next door to the White House in Kenilworth Square and not eating plaice boiled in milk on the South Circular Road.

I was back in London, talking to an old friend, Joseph Horovitz, when my grandfather's Hebrew name suddenly came to mind – Bezalel Dov. Apart from being a fine composer, Joe is a considerable Hebrew and biblical scholar. He might know what "Bezalel" meant. He did.

"It's a name in the Bible," he told me. "Exodus, I think. After Moses received the Ten Commandments, Bezalel was the man God chose to design the thing – the ark of the covenant – in which they were carried."

We looked it up. It was indeed in Exodus – Chapter 31.

"Why do you want to know?" Joe asked.

I explained that Bezalel had been my grandfather's name.

"Were there any designers in the family?" Joe asked.

I didn't think there were any in Lithuania, let alone in my family. I added that his full name was Bezalel Dov, but I knew Dov was short for David.

"It isn't," Joe said. "It means bear."

"Bare?" I said. "Like nude?"

"No. B-e-a-r. You know, the animal you meet in the jungle."

As Joe is a cosmopolitan, metropolitan person, I had to explain that he wouldn't meet any bears in a jungle. It seemed a poor exchange of knowledge compared to his about Bezalel. Still, I now knew what my grandfather's Hebrew name meant – Designer Bear. This didn't exactly bring me any closer to solving the mystery. It seemed unlikely that some Cork Immigration Officer had declared: "We can't call him Designer Bear Preuss, so let's call him Charles Beresford Price?"

I had also mentioned my grandpaternal search to Joe Briscoe, son of Robert Briscoe, the celebrated late Lord Mayor of Dublin. A retired dentist, Joe had been the longest-serving officer in the Irish Defence Force, admittedly as a military dentist. Fascinated by my quest, he wrote me six months later to say he had repeated the story to his cousin, Len Yodaiken, a Dubliner now living on Kibbutz Kfar Hanasai in Israel, whose passion was genealogy. Enclosed was a friendly letter for me from his cousin, who also had four Lithuanian grandparents, including one from Ackmeyan, who had also arrived in Cork. As regards my grandfather, Len Yodaiken wrote:

> I believe that you almost had the answer to your conundrum, but were missing a tiny bit of information. Jews in Lithuania had Hebrew names which they used in the ritual of the synagogue and Yiddish names which they used in their everyday dealings. The Hebrew "Bezalel Dov" would in Yiddish be "Tzalei Ber". The nearest the immigration officer could get to Tzalei was Charlie, and so your grandfather became "Charles Ber". The official clearly had a sense of humour, and couldn't resist an opportunity to cock a snook at the "Ascendency", so he added the "esford", and thus your grandfather became Charles Beresford. This seems to me a perfectly satisfactory explanation and I trust it is acceptable to you.

It was. Absolutely acceptable. And if there is another explanation I don't want to hear it. I am immensely grateful to Len Yodaiken, and if I can ever do him a favour, genealogical or otherwise, I will be happy to do so. For incidental interest he added:

> In general names, especially family names, were of no importance to our Jews. They were forced to take family names by the Tsar in 1825, and they mixed up their Hebrew, Yiddish and civil names in such a way as to have a different one on every document which made them difficult to locate for purposes of taxation and recruitment in the confusion of the Tsarist Empire.

This ingenious trick does raise a fascinating possibility that I've never seen taken into account before. If every Jew had three or four names to confuse the bureaucracy, it's possible that unless the bureaucrats went round personally counting, there were only a million, instead of the supposed four million, Jews in Russia. Possible, but probably not. Whatever the confusions in the Tsarist Empire, they couldn't have got it that wrong.

5.

Dublin 1957. Robert Briscoe, the new Lord Mayor of Dublin, asks the way to the Mansion House.

"No Religion"

I find it hard to distinguish between what I really remember of Charles Beresford Price in person and the tales I was told about him. Many of these were probably apocryphal. However, he clearly exercised the imaginations of his family and contemporaries. To some he was a shy, forgetful, devoutly religious man, at the mercy of his difficult daughters; to others, he resembled an obsessively religious manic-depressive with a ferocious temper, who bullied his entire family.

He started, it's said, by travelling the West of Ireland on a donkey, selling religious objects. As there was clearly no market in Connemara for prayer-shawls, *mezuzahs*, and True Splinters of the Mosaic Stone Tablets, I assume the objects he sold were Catholic. There is no record of for how long, nor how well, he did this, but by 1890 Charles Beresford was in Dublin and married to Sarah Shreider. Sarah was from a family of considerable Jewish culture, who, back in *der heim*, had been teachers and musicians. By 1897, when my father was born, the family was living in Little Jerusalem in a small terraced house near the canal, where they had a choice, in the surrounding streets, of at least five *shteibls*, those tiny, unhygienic places of worship mentioned in that 1890 circular. By then my grandfather had progressed from being a "pedlar" to "draper", which probably only signified a difference in the items he sold.

A few years later, now with two sons and three daughters, Charles Beresford had managed to buy a larger, terraced house on the South Circular Road proper, the canal still only a few yards from their small back garden. He seems to have made some money, for he had bought a pony and trap which, it's said, he drove fearlessly round the city during the euphemistically termed "Troubles". At one point, when stopped at a barricade and challenged, "Are you a Protestant or a Catholic?" "A Jew," he had replied. "Are you a Protestant Jew or a Catholic Jew?" his questioners persisted. When he again replied, "A Jew", one sentry is said to have shouted to the other: "Let him pass – no religion!"

Apocryphal or not, the story neatly sums up the position of the Irish Jew. Preoccupied as the country was by its rebellion against Britain, its subsequent Civil War, and its Protestant/Catholic and North/South divisions, the Republic had neither the time nor energy for strong reactions to a small body of recent immigrants – provided they didn't take sides. And it entirely suited the Jews not to. After the persecution of Czarist Russia, to be in a country where violence was directed against others must have been an enormous relief. However, while trying to remain uninvolved, the Jews would nevertheless have found too many parallels with their own recent past not to identify with the Catholic Irish. It would have taken no great leap of the imagination to substitute the British Empire for the Russian, or to see their own experience mirrored in that of the Irish – a largely peasant population oppressed and pauperised by often-absentee landlords, and discriminated against in nearly every aspect of national life.

The repression that followed the Easter Rising would have only emphasised the parallels, distant English prisons for remote Siberian ones, the Black and Tans standing in for Cossacks and pogroms. At Kelly's Corner, 200 yards from home, my father saw a home-made bomb tossed into the back of one of the Black and Tans' open trucks and bits of bodies flying all over the road. After several such incidents, steel meshes were installed to protect the trucks. For her part, Grandma White told us stories of IRA men running over their roof, and the Black and Tans searching their house, and, she swore, stealing their few valuables. During this period my father and his friends became firm Irish patriots, several of them either joining or helping the IRA, including Robert Briscoe, later to become a TD and Lord Mayor of Dublin.

The birth of the Free State in 1922 corresponded with my grandfather's few brief periods of prosperity. At one point in the 1920s he traded in his pony and trap for a motor car, not a big American model like the Whites', but a small Ford, one of the first cars in Little Jerusalem. There was no such thing as a driving test in the Dublin of those days, and apparently he drove the car out of the showroom after minimal verbal instructions, proceeding happily at a steady 10 mph round the town. He had only the vaguest idea that if you changed gear the car would go faster. No doubt, after a pony and trap, 10 mph seemed a perfectly fine speed – and the car kept you dry.

There seemed to be a general view that my grandfather was none too interested in worldly matters. Fortunately, for his daily devotions, Dublin's second major synagogue was being built on the site of Greenville House, directly opposite his house. For a highly orthodox Jew from Tels, having an impressive new synagogue in white stone on his very doorstep must have made Little Jerusalem seem like the Holy City itself. Once it opened, he crossed the road twice a day for the morning and evening services – until he had an angry disagreement with the wardens. It seems to have been over some minor theological matter, but such was his pride that till his death, some fifteen years later, he never entered Greenville Hall Synagogue again, walking a couple of miles to the Adelaide Road synagogue instead. This pattern of anger and pride, two characteristics deplored by his religion, was to dog his life and have catastrophic effects for his family.

Around this time, he went into hospital for an appendectomy. Hospital practice then confined patients to bed for some days after such an operation – but not my grandfather.

On the following morning he got up to say his prayers, first putting on his *tefillin*, the little boxes attached to leather thongs which the orthodox wear for morning prayers. The first of these boxes, which contain tiny scrolls with the Ten Commandments written on them, is placed on the inside of the upper arm, facing the heart. The thong is then wrapped round the forearm in seven tight loops. As my grandfather went through this rigmarole, a nurse overheard an Irishman in the next bed say to his neighbour, "Sure you've got to hand it to these Jewmen! Yer man's been in here twenty-four hours, and already he's taking his own blood-pressure!"

By this time, my father, Morris, known as Jim, would have been a medical student at the Royal College of Surgeons. He had not had an easy time getting there. After leaving school at sixteen, he had worked in a chemist's shop, studying pharmacy part-time and becoming a qualified pharmacist four years later.

Jim Price in Hayes Cunningham & Robinson chemist shop, Dublin, 1920s.

He was then able to work his way through medical school. His brother Marks, having qualified six years ahead of him, was already working as a GP in London. As soon as he qualified, my father got a job as a house surgeon at Bethnal Green, a London hospital on the fringe of the East End, which was almost entirely staffed by Irish doctors and nurses. For my father, it was like finding a congenial home abroad – but a home without family pressures.

Back in Dublin, the photographs of the period show the three sisters in their twenties, cheerful looking in bright summer-frocks. Hilda is a tall, handsome woman, Minnie smaller, and not unattractive, and Polly, larger, with thick glasses, the least attractive, but reputedly the liveliest. In a couple of the surviving photos there are even some male escorts visible.

My grandfather was a Freemason. No one knew why, but the family always said it was the cause of his downfall. They were always secretive too about the circumstances. In his brief prosperous period he had met another Freemason in Dublin, and they agreed to open a biscuit factory together. After my grandfather invested nearly all his hard-earned money in the venture, this man in some way cheated him and made off with the money. The daughters' dowries were lost. The Ford was sold. My grandmother, her health failing, retreated increasingly to bed, and my grandfather even further into religion.

With the car sold, he now faced the problem of the walk to Adelaide Road synagogue twice a day for prayers. It would have been easily resolved, had he made his peace across the road, but his pride would not allow it. Instead, he prayed at home, and he made the trek to Adelaide Road and back on Saturdays only. For work, he went back to being a tally-man, taking his samples of domestic ware round in a big brown case. His working week was not overlong. In the winter he had to be home before sunset on Friday for the arrival of the Sabbath, which lasted until an hour after sunset on Saturday. Nobody in Ireland worked on Sunday. In addition, he observed every conceivable holy day, for which a devout Jew can find a large number, including a fast to commemorate every time some new invader destroyed the Temple in Jerusalem. Add to this total the number of Saints' days when no self-respecting Catholic wants a Jew at his door selling tablecloths, let alone collecting the instalment on the curtains bought the previous week. As a result my grandfather spent quite a lot of time at home. Around this time, my father and his brother Marks must have started sending regular cheques back home – two expatriate bachelors who suddenly found themselves with more or less five dependants. This situation could not have helped either their bank balances or their own relationships.

In the summer of 1929, my Grandparents White, now well established in Rathgar, arrived on the London scene. They came on a visit with their second daughter, Gypsy, and stayed in the Regent Palace, a fine, new hotel off Piccadilly. There was a firm purpose to their trip – they were worried about their middle daughter, who was twenty-four and still unmarried. Though courted by some of Dublin's most eligible Jewish men, she seemed only interested in tennis, swimming, and driving fast cars. On top of his other business interests, Oscar White had by now opened the Standard Shoe Company, just off O'Connell Street. As his two sons were already showing signs of becoming playboys, he had hoped to interest Gypsy in its management, but to no avail.. It was the classic pattern of the second generation frittering away what the first generation had struggled to acquire.

The White family were distant cousins of the Prices from *der heim*. In Dublin they had not had much to do with each other socially, but now matters were different, as there were now two doctors in the Price family. It was well known that Jim had showed great application and perseverance in becoming a doctor, both excellent qualities in a husband. And, at thirty-two, he was only eight years older than Gypsy.

My mother often talked about the old days in what she insisted on calling "dirty old Dublin". She talked of places and people, but never of relationships. However, one evening at the age of eighty, and already widowed twelve years, we were having supper and she suddenly started talking about herself and Jim before they had married. As she talked that evening, she spoke about herself quite dispassionately, as if describing someone else – a young, rather frivolous, silly creature. She recalled how when Jim was home in Dublin from London to see his parents, he would sometimes visit the White House for tea. Her father had always insisted that she stay in to see him, whereas she wanted to go off into town or to the tennis club. Anyway he was eight years older, a doctor in London, and he was only coming to see the folks. (She always called her parents "the folks".) He wouldn't be in the least bit interested in talking to her.

"I never realised why the folks insisted on my going with them to London," she told me that night. "I thought it was just for a holiday. We all went out for dinner, and they'd asked Jim along. I don't think I thought anything more about it. I must have been very stupid. Then I remember just he and I went to the theatre. I can't remember what we saw, but coming back to the hotel in the taxi, he asked me to marry him. I just laughed."

"You just laughed!" I said incredulously. "He proposed to you and you just laughed?"

She nodded, looking rather embarrassed about how badly that young woman had behaved.

"The folks were waiting up for me when I got back to the hotel. They wanted to know what had happened. So I told them. I can never remember Daddy being so angry with me. He started shouting – What was wrong with Jim? I told him there was nothing wrong with Jim. I'd just not thought about marrying him. He thought I was totally stupid, and told me next time I spoke to Jim I should say 'Yes'. So next day I did."

I remember her words about the London visit quite vividly.

Dublin, 1930. Jim and Gypsy on their wedding day.

She had an attractive, musical voice, still with its Irish accent. I had a reminder of it quite recently. I came in, turned my answer-phone to playback, and the first message was from my mother, three years dead, the voice plaintive, "Stanley, could you phone me when you get in, I don't feel too good ..." I went cold with shock. Then I remembered the tape had been full, and instead of wiping it as I usually did, I had, for some unaccountable reason, turned it over. There would be many, many sad calls from the past on that side of the tape. Next day I bought a new one.

After she had said this much that evening, she simply switched off, as though it had finally occurred to her that she did not come well out of the story. I still have the wedding photographs – the wedding of the season in Adelaide Road synagogue, and almost the entire Jewish community of Dublin at the reception in the old Metropole Ballroom. There would have been dancing. While my mother was a fine dancer, my father was not. Slightly portly even then, he moved in a series of enthusiastic jerks, a style she could never cure him of. There is a photo of them on honeymoon, sitting on the shore of Lake Lucerne. It is summer, and they are in swimsuits, looking quite glamorous. They would have swum, she with great style, he rather as he danced – enthusiastically, but without skill, so that after half-a-dozen fierce strokes he would start to sink. They also played tennis in the same contrasting styles, her forehand and backhand elegantly produced, his an impatient, hurried swing at the ball. They came back to live in London, where her dowry helped buy him a practice in Hackney. He became a hard-working GP in a working-class district. She became a doctor's wife, and a year later I was born.

Meanwhile, back on the South Circular Road, life for the three sisters deteriorated. Their father had contributed money in his more prosperous period, to help his two sons become doctors, but in the manner of the time, had not thought it important that his daughters should receive any serious education, other than in religious matters. They would in due course get married, he thought, and all their problems would be resolved. He had not foreseen that without a dowry their attractions would be considerably reduced. However Charles Beresford Price saw no reason why his daughters should marry beneath them. Perhaps his aristocratic name had given him illusions of grandeur. Yet my mother insisted it was not only his pride, but his daughters' sharp tongues that drove away even the hardiest of suitors. As the financial situation deteriorated, the sisters became increasingly isolated in the house, looking after an increasingly invalid mother and appeasing the irascible father.

The three sisters now began to fight among themselves. From all accounts, Polly, the youngest and liveliest, was the cause of most of it. Her mood swings were beginning to rival her father's, but whereas he retreated into prayer, she advanced into hysteria. Then, in July 1940, my grandfather was diagnosed with cancer of the throat. His illness was mercifully short, and he died on the 23rd August, 1940. The house on the South Circular Road might have been calmer without him, but only for a few months.

1941 arrived with a bang. On the night of the 1st of January, a couple of bombs fell on Dublin. Given the family's current luck, it was inevitable that one of them should fall next door. Their house was damaged, but, mercifully, the only casualty was Polly, who was blown out of bed. At the time she made a joke of it, but a little later her hysterical attacks took a turn for the worse. The neighbouring house, which belonged to an assistant-rabbi, suffered more damage, but no one was actually injured. A few weeks later a bomb fell on Dublin's North Strand, killing over thirty people.

The newspapers were full of speculation about the reasons behind the bombs. Was it a warning to the Irish government to stay neutral? But then, de Valera's government had rarely showed any signs of doing otherwise. The Taoiseach was sticking still to the old political principle that Britain's misfortune was Ireland's opportunity. He did, however, after the fire-bombing of Belfast, allow some fire engines to go up and help there. Were the two bombings meant to act as a warning against further such gestures? Or was it merely a lost Luftwaffe bomber limping home, with a dead navigator, after bombing Liverpool or Manchester? Or just a callous pilot, anxious to lighten his load, and fly home a little faster? The mystery of the bombing of Dublin has never been resolved. Though the name "Little Jerusalem" was little used now, the area was still partially Jewish, and local speculation inevitably took a more paranoid turn. Why should one of the three bombs of the War land on Jewish homes? Had Hitler and his Luftwaffe some miraculous technology that could identify a Jewish home from the air, a device that could spot a *mezuzah* from 6,000 feet – and in the dark? Everyone knew the Nazis were anti-Semites, but was God also one? This question was later to arise more horrifically when the full appalling reality of the concentration camps finally emerged.

6. Everybody Knew Bloom

The damage that just one bomb could cause on the South Circular Road brought home the dangers my father faced in London. The Blitz was in full swing, and my father, just over call-up age, now looked after a vast, amalgamated practice in a heavily bombed area. My mother worried about him constantly and felt guilty about being away from him. She talked of going back for periods, and leaving Ashley and me with her parents. They dissuaded her. It was better, they said, that he come over and visit when he could.

The summer in Ireland had two great joys. The first was my father coming over for his holidays. The second was the house my grandparents White always rented at Sandycove. It was an ordinary-looking, stuccoed, 1930s-built villa, but its position was spectacular. It stood alone, sticking out slightly into the sea at the southern end of Dublin Bay. You could see it as you steamed into Dun Laoghaire harbour on the mail-boat. In front of the house was a small lawn ending in a low, stone wall and a short jetty, and beyond it the sea, stretching across the bay to Howth Head five or so miles away. On the jetty the local fishermen who unloaded their pots taught me how to hold the live lobsters, though I was never allowed to eat one. Still, their slow, sinister movements fascinated me. Like all shellfish, they are not kosher. My grandparents were quite liberal about religion, but pigs and shellfish were still beyond the Pale.

Behind the house was the celebrated Forty-Foot, a steep-sided, rocky inlet where the waves beat up against huge rocks, and the water is supposedly forty-feet deep. In fact its name came from a British regiment, the 40th Foot, stationed there in the early 19th century. It was for men only, and only very experienced swimmers were allowed in, which excluded my father and me. In the early summer mornings the place was frequented by priests from the seminary at Blackrock. One morning, passing my grandmother's bedroom at the back of the house, I heard the unusual sound of her shouting. Then Mary, the maid, came out of the bedroom crying. Liking Mary, I went in and asked my grandmother what was wrong. She looked embarrassed and mumbled something about Mary should be working and not looking out of the window. It seemed out-of-character for my grandmother to shout at someone for looking out of a window. My curiosity aroused, I went and looked out of the back window when my grandmother wasn't around. The window overlooked the great rocks of the Forty-Foot, on which all the priests were lying, naked in the early morning sun. I could tell they were priests by their tonsures.

Behind the house to the south, we were overshadowed by the Joyce Tower, the Martello Tower where the poet and surgeon Oliver St John Gogarty took up residence in 1904, renting it from the War Office for £8 per annum. His friend James Joyce came to stay from the 9th to the 15th of September. Joyce had to share these unusual digs with a visiting English drinker called Trench, who had irritatingly become more Irish than the Irish. Trench possessed a pistol and, on the night of 14th September, apparently had a nightmare about a black panther. Leaping out of bed, he opened fire on the animal, narrowly missing Joyce. A sensible valuer of his own skin, Joyce took off for Dublin next morning. Firmly fixed in his head, the scene became the opening of *Ulysses*, with Gogarty caricatured as "the stately, plump Buck Mulligan".

One of the many subjects about which Joyce and Gogarty disagreed was Jews. Gogarty was later to write several anti-Semitic articles for Arthur Griffith's *Sinn Fein*. Having read these during his stay in Rome, Joyce wrote to his brother, Stanislaus, about "Gogarty's stupid drivel". Joyce saw the Jews as a wandering, persecuted people and felt a strong affinity with them. After all, was he not himself a wandering Irishman, a persecuted writer?

I first heard of Joyce when I asked my father why the tower behind the house was named after a girl. He explained that Joyce was a great Irish writer, and that his character Leopold Bloom, the most famous character in Irish literature, was Jewish. He then went on to give me a slightly garbled account of the story of *Ulysses*. However, my father had other, more personal, connections with its author. He said he had gone to the same primary school as Joyce – the Christian Brothers on Synge Street, though some ten years later. He also claimed to know the man Joyce had used as the model for Bloom – Eugene Mushatt's father, who ran a chemist shop on Clanbrassil Street.

I had no reason to doubt my father's inside knowledge, at least not till thirty years later. Having finally read *Ulysses*, and fascinated by a writer who had been to my father's old school, I next read Richard Ellman's definitive biography of Joyce. There I found that while Joyce had briefly attended a Christian Brothers school, it was not the one on Synge Street, but rather in the poorer area of North Richmond Street. I also discovered that Bloom was not modelled on the father of my father's friend. Bloom was not even modelled on a Dublin Jew, but still my father had died convinced of his connections with a great Irish writer.

In fact it is arguable whether Bloom is even Jewish. In the novel his father, a Hungarian Jew, changes his name from Virag to Bloom when he arrives in Dublin. He also marries a Catholic, which means, according to Jewish law where the religion passes through the maternal line, their son would not be considered Jewish. In *Ulysses*, the freethinking Bloom admits that he was baptised twice as a Protestant, had converted to Catholicism, and was never circumcised. Pace my father, what

Joyce in fact created was an Everyman that anyone could call their own – Jew, Gentile, Irishman, or Hungarian.

Ellman convincingly shows how Leopold Bloom is a composite of two men: John Joyce, the author's own feckless father, and Ettore Schmitz, a Jewish businessman to whom Joyce

Bloomsday 1993. Gerald Davis as Bloom with Dermod Lynsky as James Joyce, outside the Guinness Hopstore.

Justin MacInnes

taught English in the Berlitz School in Trieste. In 1907, when Schmitz started his English lessons, Joyce was twenty-five and Schmitz forty-four. Joyce, the teacher, was an aspiring writer, while Schmitz, the pupil, a part-time novelist, would eventually achieve literary recognition as Italo Svevo, a name he took "out of pity for the one vowel surrounded by six consonants in the name Schmitz". In fact I was already a great admirer of Svevo's work when I discovered his relationship with Joyce.

Svevo was a director of his in-laws' family company which manufactured the "Moravia Anti-Fouling Composition", an anti-corrosive paint for ships. The paint had been sold to all the major navies in the huge naval build-up prior to the First World War, and Svevo needed to improve his English for business reasons. How a Triestine Italian Jew's English – as taught by James Joyce – sounded is hard to imagine. Svevo prospered, but was never happy in his work. Like Joyce, his greatest ambition was to be a full-time writer.

Joyce may have empathised with Jews, but what he knew about their religion came mainly from his reading. When he had lived in Dublin the Jewish population was around 2,000, and none of them would have mixed in the same circles as the young Joyce. Indeed there is no record of his having more than a passing acquaintance with any of them. He did borrow ten shillings from one of the Jewish Sinclair twins just before he eloped with Nora Barnacle for the Continent, though this scarcely implies a close relationship as Joyce would borrow from anybody. When he arrived in Trieste in 1905, a city he was to stay in for ten years, the Jewish population was around 6,500, and active in all walks of life. Though brought up in traditional Judaism, Svevo himself had totally lapsed and was married to a Catholic. He was, however, well versed in the social and religious aspects of being a Jew, and Joyce picked his brains mercilessly. Later, when Svevo met Joyce's brother, Stanislaus, he told him, "Tell me some secrets about Irishmen. I want to get even with your brother."

Joyce read Svevo's novels, written in the Triestine dialect and virtually ignored by the public and the literary establishment, and admired both their content and the subtly ironic style. He also gave Svevo the first three chapters of *Portrait of the Artist as a Young Man*, the project on which he had been stuck for over a year. In a long letter, Svevo offered praise and constructive criticism. The two men were to encourage and help each other over the next twenty years. Their relationship always retained a rather quaint formality, a tone set more by Joyce than the worldly Svevo. Traces of Joyce's puritanical Dublin upbringing remained, and he once berated Svevo for an off-colour joke, remarking "I never say that sort of thing though I write it". Commenting later to a friend, Svevo said, "It would appear then that Joyce's works are not ones that could be read in his own presence."

Joyce was already planning *Ulysses* during his early relationship with Svevo, and Bloom would eventually emerge with several of Svevo's characteristics. Both are lapsed Jews who have gone through conversions of convenience; both are in their mid-forties and married to Catholics. Bloom is also endowed with the amiably ironical outlook that Svevo displayed in his life and in his books. When *Ulysses* was finally published in its entirety in Paris in 1922, Joyce was able to use his new celebrity to help his old Triestine pupil, whose last book *Confessions of Zeno* had been privately published in Italy and largely ignored. Joyce used his influence to circulate the book among the Parisian literati, who hailed it as a masterpiece. It was published in France in 1926 to the highest praise and Svevo was lionised in literary circles for the last few years of his life.

If Svevo was the first Jew Joyce encountered at close quarters, he subsequently became friendly with many more, writers, critics, artists, and musicians, as he moved between Trieste, Zurich, and Paris. As an intellectual class, he was fascinated by their complexities and contradictions. Joyce obviously saw parallels with his own early immersion and then rejection of Catholicism in so many of these friends, who had themselves experienced but rejected conventional Judaism. As an Irishman in exile, Joyce lived as much in a diaspora as those European Jews with whom he mixed, whereas in the England or Ireland of the day he would never have found that sort of intellectual or bohemian Jew. One of Joyce's non-Jewish friends, the Swiss critic, Jacques Mercanton, once asked him why Leopold Bloom had to be Jewish. Joyce replied, "Only a foreigner would do. The Jews were foreigners at that time in Dublin. There was no hostility towards them, but contempt, yes, the contempt that people always show towards the unknown."

Apart from his many male friends, Joyce was greatly attracted to certain types of Jewish women whose looks he considered "oriental and voluptuous" and whose personalities he thought exotic. In Trieste he conceived a passion for one of his Jewish pupils, Amalia Popper. Though his passion went unrequited, Signorina Popper was to help him in other ways. Her voluptuousness was to serve as a model for Molly Bloom, and her English was good enough, twenty-five years later, to enable her to translate his *Dubliners* into Italian. The name Bloom, however, comes from elsewhere. In Joyce's time in Dublin there were several Jewish men of that name, one of whom was a dentist whom Joyce may have visited. Like the thriftiest of housewives, Joyce recycled everything. There were no leftovers in his literary life.

Joyce's later relationship with things Jewish developed a bitter irony that would have appealed to his sadly departed friend, Svevo. His son, Giorgio, married Helen Kastor Fleischman, an American Jew. Joyce was delighted when his only grandchild, Stephen, was born. In Judaic law, Stephen would be considered Jewish, and Joyce joked that they didn't know whether to baptise or circumcise him. In fact, the freethinking Joyce was strongly opposed to baptism and was not told till some years later that Stephen had been secretly baptised. For her part, his daughter, Lucia, was constantly attracted to Jewish men after she developed schizophrenia, fortunately not a normal condition of that illness.

The final irony occurred when Joyce attempted to escape to Switzerland from Vichy France in 1941 with Nora, their son Giorgio, and grandson Stephen. By now Giorgio had separated from his wife Helen, who was in a psychiatric clinic in America, while his sister Lucia was resident in another in France. The Zurich authorities, who had never heard of James Joyce, refused to grant him a visa on the grounds that he was a Jew. When Joyce was informed of this, he said "*C'est le bouquet, vraiment.*" His Swiss friends now rallied around. Mercanton swore a deposition that Joyce was not a Jew. Joyce, never one to miss a word-play, wrote to Swiss friends, "*Je ne suis pas juif de Judee mais aryen d'Erin.*" Eventually, the Swiss authorities demanded money – the extortionate sum of 50,000 Swiss francs, which Joyce did not have. A Jewish friend in Zurich negotiated it down to 20,000 francs, which was contributed by two other Jewish friends, one local, the other from New York. The Joyces were allowed back into Zurich, thirty-six years after they had first arrived. Joyce died there two months later. He was buried in the cemetery next to the zoological gardens, which he had once said reminded him of the zoo in Phoenix Park. Nora occasionally brought friends to see the grave. "He was awfully fond of the lions," she said to one. "I like to think of him lying there and listening to them roar." Nora herself stayed on, and died there in 1951.

I have not yet visited Zurich, to see the grave and hear the lions, but whenever I am in Dublin I go to Sandycove. I look at our old summer house, walk up behind to the Joyce Tower, and always feel deeply grateful that Trench's shot at the phantom panther missed my father's would-be schoolmate.

7. The Sandycove Rebellion

There is another reason, totally unconnected with Joyce, why I remember that Sandycove house with such affection. In 1942, when the Blitz appeared to be over, my father decided that it was safe for us all to go back to London. My mother was delighted. My brother Ashley was just three, and I had no idea what his feelings were, but I was perfectly happy where I was. Attending a small and cheerful prep school down the road and being generally fussed over by my grandmother, other relatives, and staff. Perhaps my father thought that this regimen was not good for me, and a father figure was needed instead. Not that he would ever have used such an expression – the word that would have rather sprung to his mind was discipline. Like most of his generation, even in the medical profession, he took an old-fashioned view of what is now referred to by that sickly word – parenting.

I never discovered how he felt about his own father, but, whatever his feelings, my father had never rebelled against his strictly religious upbringing. He also knew my maternal relatives took a more relaxed view of religious matters, so the idea of my long-term upbringing in Dublin would have worried him. Moreover the religious question was interwoven with another perennial problem – the rich maternal versus the poor paternal side of our family.

My father always treated money with suspicion. Money spoilt people. "If you think money makes you happy," he would say, "just look at rich people." Were we in a car together, he would illustrate this by pulling up at the lights beside a Rolls or Mercedes. Nudging me, he would say "Gib a kuk at yer man" – Litvak-Irish-Yiddish for "Take a look at that fellow" – as he gestured at some miserable-looking millionaire behind the wheel of his custom-built Bentley.

I didn't like to point out that people, even kindly poor people, often look miserable when they're driving and have to stop at lights. I didn't like to nudge him and say "Gib a kuk at who's sitting next to yer man", most often a glamorous, curvaceous blonde. Nor did I like to accuse him of being sentimental about the old-style poverty and religion back in Little Jerusalem. What rows he had with my mother were invariably about how extravagant she was, and spoilt because her parents had money. And he was determined that wouldn't happen to his children.

In any event, it had been decided, without consultation with the interested party, that I needed some continuing education of both a secular and religious nature, with some old-style discipline thrown in for good measure. To my parents this combination meant boarding school. They must have clearly felt they could afford it, and if my mother and brother had to leave London again I at least would be safely stowed away, having a proper English education. The fact that my father insisted I must eat kosher food and keep all the other religious observances did not give them great choice among English Public Schools. However, there were two schools that had Jewish boarding houses attached. Clifton, near Bristol, was full, so I ended up in Hillel House at the Perse School in Cambridge. I hated the place, and in no time at all was suffering a severe identity crisis.

Aged eleven, with a mild Irish accent, and used to the fairly undivided attention of my mother and the general friendliness of Irish people, I suddenly found myself immersed in the schizophrenic role of a Jew at an English public school. The House was a rundown, draughty, old building, and with the lethal combination of rationing and English institutional cooking, the kosher food ghastly and inadequate. And nobody there, except the English master, had ever heard of James Joyce. All there was in plenty was discipline. The housemaster was a benign old man who left that side of things to an energetic and sadistic house-tutor, who beat boys for almost any offence, without even the excuse of being an anti-Semite. Rather he was a Jew, a Jewish Jew-beater, a phenomenon I was brought up to believe never existed.

One particularly painful beating left me with prickly pains in the hip that my father diagnosed as fibrositis. He was very angry but did nothing about it. He was reticent about complaining at the best of times, and, in wartime, places at schools in safe areas were at a premium – and those safe *and* kosher, pure gold dust

The school itself seemed a big and alien place. Top of my hate list was the institution of separate prayers. During assembly in the big hall Jewish boys were confined to an adjacent classroom, but separate prayers did not mean that we said our prayers simultaneously. Rather we had already done that on pre-breakfast stomachs back at the House, so we sat in the classroom putting the finishing touches to our homework. When Christian prayers were finished in the hall, a prefect was dispatched to bring on the Jews. The doors were flung open, and on we came like a self-conscious, poorly rehearsed chorus-line to face a four hundred-strong Aryan audience. There were about thirty of us, as we went to join the ranks of our respective forms sitting cross-legged on the floor.

Entering adolescence, the last thing any pimply Jewish youth wanted was to be singled out as different, so different as to be excluded from what went on in the hall. Were they talking about us? Was the headmaster, a terrifying man nearer seven-foot than six, the tallest man I'd seen to date, telling them about the blood libel? Would there be boos and cat-calls when we self-consciously filed in, a barrage of bad eggs and rotten vegetables?

Was this to be the start of the Perse pogrom? Being forced to feel different is conducive to a lively paranoia. Till then, all that anti-Semitism had meant was my mother not being allowed to play tennis in Kenilworth Square.

As a result, I was provoked by all this into considering, for the first time, the label I wanted, rather than the one "they" were trying to give me. My initial approach was purely negative. I didn't want to be an English Jew coming through that door at an English Public School. Did I want to be English? I looked at the staff and boys in that hall and decided – definitely not. I preferred the people where I'd come from. They were friendlier, less threatening, less blandly blonde. Did I want to be a Jew? That was more difficult. The religious part entailed an endless series of regulations and proscriptions. They only made sense if you truly believed that God wanted you to do them all. I did believe in God at eleven-and-a-half, some eighteen months before my barmitzvah, but I was increasingly doubtful about all his nit-picking demands.

Would I rather be an Irish Catholic? I'd already had to consider that carefully before coming back to England, having done something in Dublin of which I was very ashamed. The event had occurred when I was about ten and first allowed to travel alone on a tram. I was feeling very adult and independent on the top deck, rattling into town, when we passed the big church on the Rathmines Road. Outside the church was the crucifix with a life-size Christ nailed on it. Everyone on the top deck devoutly crossed themselves, and so did I. I had never done it before, but from observation, I knew the drill. I would never have dared if I was with my mother or aunts, but the minute I was on my own I betrayed both them and my religion. The cock hadn't even crowed thrice, and there I was crossing myself, desperate to be like everybody else. I knew it was treacherous and wrong – that you don't leave one religion and scuttle off to another just to feel comfortable on a Dublin tram. In the end I decided I would settle for being an Irish Jew, but definitely not one in exile in the Jewish house of an English Public School. That was the worst of all possible worlds.

Nevertheless I stuck out the year at the Perse, never enjoying or adjusting to it. Scholastically I was totally at sea, as nothing I had learned in Ireland tied in with what I was being taught in England. The major gaps in my knowledge sapped my confidence. All I enjoyed was the introduction to rugby and athletics. I found I could go very fast over short distances. A hare at a 100 yards, I turned into a tortoise at any longer distance. The sadistic House tutor organised the Hillel House cross-country runs on Sundays when the non-Jewish boarders went to church. He enjoyed making us run when the weather was at its worst, the roads and fields iciest, the wind whipping in across the Fens straight from Siberia. The dayboys were still snug in their beds, waiting for their mothers to call them down to a cooked breakfast, the Christian boarders warm in their chapel singing their happy hymns, while we, poor Jews, regardless of age or infirmity, were off battling the elements on the Gog Magog Hills, surviving the stitch, and enduring that loathsome bastard of an anti-Semitic Jew screaming at us to run faster.

In the summer holiday we went back to the house at Sandycove. My father managed to spend two weeks with us. Tactfully, I waited a few days before bringing up the question of how much I hated boarding school. Calm and calculating, I played on my continuing fibrositis, on how bad my reports were, largely due to hopeless teaching, and how I didn't like the other boys, Jew or Gentile. This last line of argument was a mistake, allowing my father to turn it back on me. Maybe they didn't like me because I was being unlikeable. He supposed I got into fights with everybody. One of the teachers had actually commented on my report that my time in Ireland had certainly taught me how to be a rebel. At the time that was considered dry, English humour, rather than a politically motivated, racist attack.

My parents' responses were equally calm and calculating. I would soon get used to the school and start enjoying it. Then I would feel the benefits of a good English education, and one day I would thank them for it. What's more the War was still on, Hitler wasn't beaten yet, don't think he hadn't something up his sleeve. I would always be safe in Cambridge. At that point I lost patience and shouted what about an invasion? What about paratroopers? Wasn't East Anglia the first place they'd drop in on? I don't remember my parents' reply. By 1943 they would have known, in some detail, what the Nazis were doing to Jews on the Continent. I knew about Hitler not liking Jews, that it would be better for us if we didn't have to fight him on the beaches, fields, and streets. But what was really happening across the Channel was never discussed in front of me. The subject of a German invasion and my returning to boarding school was dropped. My mother took me aside to remind me that my father was returning to the poor, sick, bombed people of Hackney, and he shouldn't be upset – "He's got enough to worry about!" It was a frequent heart-felt cry that I never took seriously enough.

My father returned to the sick of Hackney. I stayed on to cycle, swim, and pick up live lobsters in the shadow of the Joyce Tower. One morning, looking at the waves beating up against the rocks of the Forty Foot, I decided, with a sudden flash of clarity, I would not go back to Hillel House. If they thought my time in Ireland had taught me to be a rebel, then I would show them how right they were. I dreamed up my own summer equivalent of the Easter Rising. Most of the summer holiday still lay ahead of me to plan it, while eating all the meat, fish, eggs, and fresh butter I wanted. The only things Ireland in "the Emergency" did not have were white flour and coal. If we ate a rather indigestible brown bread, I grew to love the smell of burning peat billowing out of the chimneys of houses and trains.

I waited for inspiration, for the little people in the green pointy hats to whisper in my ear. When the time came the little people whispered on cue. On the morning of my departure, after breakfast, I went into the upstairs bathroom, which also contained the main toilet, and locked myself in with my omnibus edition of Sherlock Holmes. I would not come out till I had assurances of not having to go back to boarding school. My mother first laughed, then cajoled, then got angry. Already halfway through *A Study in Scarlet* I remained polite but adamant. After a brief silence on the other side of the door, my Grandma White launched into a heavily accented peroration on how parents knew best for their children and only did things for their children's good. She reminded me of the Fifth Commandment about honouring one's father and mother. That particularly applied to me, she said, because I had wonderful parents, and I shouldn't upset them. I should be good to my mother because she was lonely away from my father. My father was lonely in London. He was not just a doctor, he was a fine man, a saint, a true *mensch*. I should be so lucky as to grow up like him. As she became increasingly emotional her English shaded off into Russian and Yiddish. I should have *rachmonas*. The Germans had no *rachmonas*. Catholic anti-Semites had no *rachmonas*. I should have *rachmonas* for my parents. The word best translates as "compassion". I was nice to her through the door because I had been told that she was slowly going blind. I told her I didn't want to upset anybody. I just didn't want to go back to that horrible English school.

It went quiet again, while they regrouped their forces. Next up on the other side of the door was my easy-going Uncle Michael, my mother's younger brother. On the death of my grandfather, Michael had inherited the family shoe business, buying out his brother Arthur who, wanting a more adventurous life, had gone off to join the RAF. Uncle Michael tried to conduct an informal, affable chat through the locked bathroom door, something along the lines of "Look, old feller, you know I'm on your side, but let's be reasonable. Come out, have some lunch, and we'll talk about it …" I assured him that under no circumstances would I emerge without absolute, cast-iron guarantees that I would not be sent back. Before long he was reduced to the tired old "If you go back you'll get used to it and enjoy it soon" line of argument. He told me that was what he'd had to do. He hadn't enjoyed his new school. "Was it a boarding school?" I asked. "No," he replied lamely, his argument shot out of the water. Shortly afterwards he retreated, and it went quiet again. I could hear the downstairs toilet being used frequently. By now it was lunchtime, but I wasn't hungry or thirsty. My confidence was growing, and *The Hound of the Baskervilles* had me, with the seat down, on the edge of the toilet.

Apparently it was my Uncle Michael's idea that my mother should phone my father in London. It is odd now to think how reluctant people were to make a "trunk call". It was expensive and implied something very serious had to be imparted. By then, however, the siege was in its fourth hour, and my mother and grandmother needed things from the bathroom. Lunchtime had been and gone, but I was too terrified by the braying hounds to feel hungry. There was some trouble getting hold of my father at his surgery. He was out on his visits, but he called back in mid-afternoon, by which time I'd been in the bathroom over five hours. Years later my Uncle Michael admitted how impressed he had been by my determination to stay in the bathroom, if need be till the end of the war. He had told my father that anyone with that much determination had to have a genuine grievance. Eventually my father agreed that they could promise me that I wouldn't have to go back. My mother came to break the news. I suspected a trap, and it wasn't till Uncle Michael had also sworn on his honour that I emerged with only *The Sign of Four* and *The Valley of Fear* still to go.

A Jewish boy is meant to pass into manhood at barmitzvah, aged thirteen. Yet when mine was celebrated a year later, it meant very little to me. My real rite of passage had occurred in that magic time in the toilet of the house in Sandycove. There I had discovered that if you really put your mind to it you could defeat an adult world that always claimed to know what was best for you. I had gone into that toilet an oppressed boy at a beastly boarding school, and had come out a free man.

A quick family conference took place, and it was decided that Wesley College would be the best place for me. It was situated on St Stephen's Green in the centre of Dublin, and I could travel there on my own by tram from Rathgar. It was a Methodist day school with a reputation for religious tolerance. There were other Jewish boys there. Unlike James Joyce, who hadn't quite gone to my father's school, George Bernard Shaw had really gone to Wesley. He entered in 1865, attending rather intermittently for three years. Recalling the school in 1928, he wrote to another Old Wesleyan, "I have not a good word to say for it. It could not even teach Latin; and it never seriously tried to teach anything else – my curse on it. Forget it." The school must have changed a little in those eighty years, for despite the Shavian curse, I enjoyed it enormously.

It was during a school holiday from Wesley that my cousin, Monty, proposed we cycle out to Powerscourt where he had heard some British company were making a film. Powerscourt is a magnificent stately home and gardens about fourteen miles outside Dublin, then owned by the Slazenger family. I had never cycled that far before but because Monty was six years older than I, my mother gave her permission. There was little need for her to be concerned. Because of the acute shortage of petrol there were virtually no cars on the road and one could only have an accident with another bicycle. Monty was very vague about what film it was as we cycled out, but he knew there were some big film stars in it. When we got there, spread out in the vast green expanses of Powerscourt was the most amazing sight I had ever seen – what seemed like armies of men in medieval armour with colourfully saddled horses and others in less grand clothing who were clearly meant to be infantry. All around them, other men in present-day clothing were busying themselves with cameras and all manner of other equipment. Everyone appeared to be doing something but we couldn't work out exactly what. We joined a group of spectators where a knowledgeable local told us they hadn't started shooting yet. "They'd be lucky to get any done before lunch," he said, pointing out one of the actors in bright silver chain-mail with a scarlet surcoat and no helmet. "That's Laurence Olivier. He's directing it too." I'd never heard of him, but he did seem to be rushing around more than the other actors.

Of course I didn't realise it at the time but, in 1943, in a field fourteen miles outside Dublin, we had stumbled on the shooting of one of the greatest scenes in film history – the charge of the French knights at Agincourt in *Henry V*. We were totally mesmerised by what was going on, as the French knights mounted, put on their helmets, and began to get in line. "They're all local men who can ride," our knowledgeable local told us. The sun then went in and they broke for lunch. We ate our sandwiches and drank lemonade. Clearly the French knights had drunk something stronger, because after lunch things started going wrong. As the charge was being lined up various knights fell off their horses. A lot of their armour seemed to be made of cardboard and required running repairs. Every time they seemed ready to charge something else went wrong, a knight fell again, a horse bolted, someone lost their helmet. "Ah well," said our local informant, "they wouldn't want it over too quickly. They're earning a bloody fortune." With the inevitable stop-go, stop-go nature of filming, even without local drinking habits, we obviously weren't going to see the French knights in their ill-fated charge, let alone the English bowmen taking aim. So we cycled home, somewhat mystified by how films got made.

A year later I saw *Henry V* in a London cinema. I couldn't believe it. The film held me spellbound from the moment that sheet of paper spiraled down out of the blue sky into the open

Globe Theatre. The sound of Shakespeare, the voice of Olivier, the stylised beauty of the sets were a revelation, but most amazing of all was the battle scene. Out of that chaotic mess of men and horses I had witnessed far away in a green field came this wonderful charge – all the knights perfectly in line, starting slowly, cantering, trotting faster and faster, and then surging into that furious gallop to the soaring accompaniment of William Walton's magnificent music. There and then I fell in love with films.

The other passion that took root at Wesley was rugby football. I played wing-forward for the Under-13 XV, and particularly looked forward to away games. The names of the schools we played had an almost mystical ring to them, maybe because so many of them were named after saints – St Andrew's, St Mary's, St Columba's. There was Mountjoy, beside the sinister prison, Portora Royal, Clongowes Wood, the Jesuit school housed in a medieval castle, where Joyce stayed till his father went broke, and Belvedere, a cluster of fine 18th-century buildings in the centre of town, where Joyce had finished his schooldays. Apart from the huge tea afterwards, my delight at these fixtures might also have stemmed from the fact that most of these schools were boarding – and I had the feeling that a Catholic boarding establishment might be every bit as grim as a Jewish one. I didn't gloat over the poor boarders in the opposing scrum; they were just happy reminders of my now priviledged position as a day-boy.

The time had also come for my initiation into Irish sectarian violence. The big annual Derby was between Methodist Wesley and Catholic Blackrock. Blackrock College was attached to the Seminary, whose priests draped themselves over the rocks of the Forty Foot in all weathers. No doubt this practice is what made them so tough in body and soul, and they wanted the fine young Catholics they taught to be the same – especially when they played Protestants at rugby. Furthermore, the wrought-iron gates and stately grounds of the college were enormously impressive to a twelve-year-old. There had been too much of a build-up, so that we were already in an over-awed, highly nervous state before we even saw the size of our ferocious-looking opponents. Not one of them looked under-13. Rather they all looked as though they'd been shaving and body-building for years. Our team of tolerant, pygmy non-conformists was clearly going to be eaten alive. It crossed my mind in the changing-room, before the potential bloodbath began, to get word to their changing-room that the opposing blind-side wing-forward was Jewish. I then remembered the old, probably apocryphal, Grandpa Price line, "Are you a Catholic Jew or a Protestant Jew?" Having already decided to be an Irish Jew, I realised I was going to have to be man enough to die as a Protestant. The Catholic giants ran onto the pitch, and before the priestly referee blew for the kick-off, they all crossed themselves. Now, as well as the ref, they had God on their side.

The game went badly for me from the start. Nervous and over-eager, I broke fast from a scrum to tackle their fly-half, as a good wing-forward should. The whistle went. I was deemed offside, and a penalty was awarded. The fly-half, back on his huge feet, kicked the penalty with ease. He would no doubt have kicked the ball into Dublin if asked. I had given away three easy points. Now, as far as the Blackrock fanatics were concerned, I was a cheat as well as a heretic who had to be watched. And watched I was – with elbows, shoulders, and boots. Every time I attempted another David-Goliath encounter with their fly-half, I found Goliath's triplet brothers in my way, and if ever I got the ball they jumped on me with the precision of a circus act. After a couple more kamikaze attempts, I slacked off, and let the true-born-and-bred Protestants die valiantly for their faith.

When I got home, Grandma White took a look at my cut and bruised face and collapsed, linguistically, into Russian and Yiddish. She shouted for my mother who became equally upset in English. They said I would never play rugby again – it was a game for barbarians. Years later I discovered that one of the great honours of rugby was to be invited to play for the Barbarians. Next day at school no one talked about the terror of the previous afternoon. Bruised and limping, fifteen of us bragged that if we'd had a little more luck, and if the ref had been one of ours and not one of theirs, we could have thumped them. Wait till next year, they said. Secretly I thought how next year their Under-13s would be their Under-14s, even more immense and probably bearded. Of course, if my mother and grandmother had had their way, I wouldn't be playing any more.

On reflection, though, my mother possibly had a more considered thought. I was a rebellious child, and she had a short fuse. Ours was a combustible relationship. When, not infrequently, she lost her temper she would hit me with anything that came to hand. Maybe she thought it better that I got rid of my rebelliousness on the rugby field. And if fifteen junior Jesuits from Blackrock, Belvedere, or wherever, wanted to beat the living daylights out of me, it saved her the bother. On the other hand, to be Talmudic, for a good Jewish mother to beat her child is one thing for someone else to do it is a capital offence. In any event, I continued playing rugby, dreaming of the day when I would pull on the emerald-green shirt and run on at Lansdowne Road, hands tucked firmly in my pockets, while the others busily crossed themselves. What's more, I soon met someone who had done just that.

8. Richard And Elizabeth

Dr Bethel Solomons's name was spoken of with awe in our family, as an example of what a Jew could achieve in Irish society. One of the first Jews to qualify in medicine from Trinity College, Dublin, he went on to become a distinguished obstetrician and the 26th Master of the Rotunda, which was founded in 1745 as Europe's first purpose-built maternity hospital. However, it was not his medical skills alone that had enabled Bethel Solomons to reach the pinnacle of a profession that for other Irish Jewish medics often remained an alien environment. The further clue to his success appears in the announcement in *The Times* of May, 1946:

> Dr Bethel Solomons, who has been elected President of the Royal College of Physicians of Ireland, played Rugby for Ireland ten times.

To play for your country was to be turned into an instant hero, regardless of your religious label. Solomons was capped between 1908 and 1910, at a time when first-class sporting gentlemen with slim academic pretensions were welcomed into the older British universities, and their paths eased towards their final degrees.

My father delighted in the story of one such Irish hero, the great Jamie Clinch. Clinch had failed his medical exams several times, and if he didn't pass this particular anatomy viva, even Trinity would have had to throw him out. Anxious to win another rugby cup, the Trinity examiners limited themselves to the most basic questions, and they breathed a sigh of relief when he correctly identified a bone as a femur. Then one examiner, clearly inadequately briefed, asked "Could you tell us, Mr Clinch, is it a right femur or a left femur?" There was a long pause before Mr Clinch replied "Ah come on now, I'm not going for honours."

This is not to say that Bethel Solomons's position in the Irish medical firmament was not fully justified. An exceptional obstetrician, he won many prizes and international distinctions; if being Jewish was not exactly an advantage in the hierarchical levels of medicine at the time, playing rugby for your country undoubtedly was. His eminence as a respected figure in smart, professional Dublin society, together with his not seeking in any way to hide his Jewishness, seemed to validate the entire small Jewish community. They positively basked in his distinction.

Bethel Solomons was on the board that examined my father in midwifery and obstetrics, and his signature is on my father's graduation certificate. And it was on one of my father's brief wartime trips to Dublin, when we were walking down the west side of St Stephen's Green that he suddenly gripped my arm and hissed, "That's Bethel Solomons." A very big man was coming towards us. Solomons was about sixty then, tall, upright, thick silver hair, a very square jaw, almost a caricature of a distinguished, ex-rugby-playing consultant. Recognising my father, he said, "Morris Price." It was the first time I'd ever heard anyone call my father that, not "Jim". They shook hands and talked about the War and what my father was doing in London. When I was introduced, Solomons asked what school I was at. Wesley, I said. A good rugby school, he said. Did I play? Yes. For the Under-13s. What position, he asked. Wing forward. He said I had the right build for it. He patted my shoulder and told me he'd be looking out for me at Landsdowne Road one day. We shook hands all round and parted. To have been patted on the shoulder by Bethel Solomons on St Stephen's Green was better than any apostolic blessing or its Jewish equivalent. "He's a grand man, is Bethel," my father said, positively glowing as we walked up into Grafton Street.

Twenty-five years later, Bethel Solomons's name came up again in extraordinary circumstances. I was in Bray, where my mother had once won the Ladies' high-diving championship. At Ardmore Studios nearby, *The Spy Who Came In From the Cold* with Richard Burton was being shot, and an American magazine had commissioned me to interview him and write a piece about the filming.

Notebook and ballpoint at the ready I was ushered into the star's dressing-room. I found myself in the presence of the world's most famous couple. Elizabeth Taylor, between film jobs, was visiting her then-husband. However I did not instantly and irrevocably fall in love with her, thereby ruining the rest of my life. Her violet eyes were indeed strikingly beautiful, but she was well known for putting on weight between jobs, and she was between jobs. She was also badly in need of a hairdresser. I knew from previous journalistic jobs that meeting film stars was frequently a disappointing aesthetic experience. One is used to seeing them at their best on the screen, larger-than-life and perfectly made-up. In the flesh they usually turn out smaller than expected, blotchier-complexioned and inevitably wilder-haired. This was the 60s when a hair out-of-place meant a re-take. However Burton, about to go on, had everything perfectly in place, and looked and sounded in great shape. The pair of them were charming, if a little preoccupied. They offered me a drink and then excused themselves, as they needed to sort out some complicated arrangements concerning servants and animals. Mrs Burton seemed deeply worried about her dogs, which were in private quarantine on their yacht, parked somewhere on the Thames. There were also some staff problems at the house in Italy. In fact the world's most famous couple were running up a huge international telephone bill in front of my very eyes. I wasn't getting much of an interview but felt flattered that, on such brief acquaintance, they were willing to let me share their complex domestic lives. Burton was then summoned to the set. His wife was still on the phone to LA, about some refurbishment to their home there, so the publicist suggested that I might like to have tea and chat to the writer of the film.

The publicist also mentioned that the screenwriter on this film was, unusually, also the author of the original novel. Accordingly I was shown into a small box room that contained a table, a typewriter, and John Le Carré. It became perfectly clear to me, after one mouthful of tea, that this was a deeply depressed writer. After a chocolate digestive, he admitted as much. He had only recently left the Foreign Office to concentrate on writing and had had no success till this book. Yet just when he could have been taking his ease, or getting on with another novel, he had made the fatal mistake of agreeing to write the screenplay, rather than entrust it to somebody else.

At this stage in my writing life, I had also written a couple of less than best-selling novels. Peter Sellers had optioned one for £200 and never made it into a film. Later, I was to discover from other writers that for Sellers this was common practice. It happened that I too would rather have been at home writing another novel than waiting there to talk to the Burtons, but, like a good journalist, I suppressed my hard-luck story and listened to his. Le Carré had already written endless drafts of the screenplay before they went into production, but now the director, Marty Ritt, had brought him back to make more changes even as they were filming. Each batch of rewrites went on to different coloured pages, and Le Carré could no longer remember whether he was on blue or green, or whether the whole gamut of colours had been run and he was back to white again. He vowed that he would never work on a screenplay again, and he never has. Later, when I myself had been seduced for a period into film writing, and was on my umpteenth lot of coloured pages, I often wished I had heeded that warning in the box room at Ardmore.

The next day I watched some of the film being shot but came no nearer getting an interview. Another crisis had come up. This time it was over the Burtons' chauffeur, Gaston, who was their veritable shadow, a dark and wiry Corsican with slicked-back hair and a black leather coat. Looking like a cross between a Mafiosa and a Gestapo officer, he spoke English with the charm and accent of Maurice Chevalier. Having brought their Bentley over from England, he had, one evening driving down O'Connell Street, run into and injured a small boy. A court case was looming, but the Burtons were trying their best to achieve an out-of-court settlement. I would have thought a sensible interim measure for the authorities would have been to ban Gaston from Irish roads. Obviously no such thought had occurred to them, and that afternoon, at breakneck speed, he drove Elizabeth Taylor and me back into Dublin. As there had again been no chance of talking to Mr Burton that afternoon, Mrs Burton had offered me a lift back into town. I was conscious, as we sat together in the back of the car, that she had been to the hairdresser and was wearing some very agreeable perfume. She hadn't lost any weight, but I was beginning to overlook that. As we came speeding into town, I noticed people looking at the car and thought of a variation on the old Pope and Mr Goldberg joke – "Who's that sitting next to Stanley Price?" I would have liked to have been seen by someone I knew, preferably a relative, though not Aunts Minnie or Hilda – probably the only two people in Dublin who had never heard of Elizabeth Taylor.

The next day, a Saturday, back at Ardmore Studios, the publicist assured me that after a little morning shooting Mr Burton would definitely have time to be interviewed. At midday I went to his dressing room yet again. Richard and Liz – for by now we were on very familiar terms – were there. The champagne was uncorked and the television on. It was Winston

Churchill's funeral, live, so to speak, from London. As the coffin was taken up the Thames by barge, Burton showed me the cufflinks that had been given to him personally by Churchill. Burton had frequently imitated Churchill's voice for television and radio documentaries, and Churchill had given him the gift in appreciation. Then, as the coffin was transferred from the barge to the gun-carriage for the last mile to St Paul's, Burton did a brilliant impersonation of Churchill commentating on his own funeral, drowning out the pious platitudes of Richard Dimbleby. Liz cried. We drank more champagne. Richard cried. I thought it would be churlish not to join in. That was another day I didn't get an interview.

Finally, my hour came. One of the sets had fallen apart, and Burton had an unscheduled afternoon off. Gaston drove us to a hotel in the Dublin mountains. It was a memorable lunch. Over the first course we discovered our mutual passion for rugby, and that was that. He had total recall of the great moments of Welsh rugby. For a while I countered with some instances of Irish genius, but by dessert he had the floor to himself. From a sitting position behind a strawberry mousse he recaptured Haydn Tanner's exquisite inside jink. With the merest shrug of his shoulders, he was Bleddyn Williams selling the superb dummy that wrong-footed the entire English defence at the Arms Park. At any minute I felt he would break into *Sospen Fac*, and the entire entranced, eavesdropping dining room would join in. Then, over an almost penultimate whiskey, he told me where he was taking Liz that evening. They were going out to dinner to meet a great Irish rugby hero – not any old Irish rugby hero, but an Irish Jewish rugby hero, Dr Bethel Solomons. Had I ever heard of him? I told Burton how, with my father, I had met him twenty-three years before. But, Burton asked, did I know the famous story about Bethel when he was in the Irish team beaten by Wales at Lansdowne Road? My father had told it to me at least half-a-dozen times, but I said I didn't know it. I reckoned Richard Burton would probably tell it at least as well as my Dad.

The great Welsh voice launched itself again, with a total command of a Dublin brogue when necessary. It was one of Ireland's biggest defeats at Landsdowne Road. The Irish crowd was disconsolate, and their team, ashamed and probably terrified, remained in the changing-room till most of their erstwhile fans had dispersed. Finally Bethel Solomons emerged to overhear two lamenting Irish supporters. "Have you ever seen an Irish team play like that before?" said the first. To which the other replied, "Call that an Irish team – fourteen Protestants, and one feckin' Jew!"

The story differed only by one word from my father's version – my father had said "bloody" rather than "feckin". Burton then went on to give the reason why Liz should meet Bethel Solomons. He wanted her to meet a real Jew. She only knew American showbiz Jews like Mike Todd, Sammy Davis Jr, and Marilyn Monroe. I didn't point out that the last two were converts like Liz herself. I didn't question his definition of Bethel Solomons as "a real Jew", and I wasn't quite drunk enough to offer to introduce Liz to some really "real Jews" on the South Circular Road. We parted, swearing we would go to an eternity of international rugby matches together. We never did, and I never found out how Liz got on with Bethel Solomons. However, I did see in the papers that Gaston was let off with a caution, after an out-of-court settlement for damages had been agreed.

As always after journalistic forays into celebrity territory, I went back gratefully to my own life. I told my wife how fortunate we were not to have houses, cars and yachts, dogs and cats, chauffeurs and other servants. I assured her that all such things do is give you endless problems and huge phone bills. I told her that, all right, she didn't quite have Liz's eyes, but her figure and hair were in better shape.

"But *she* got the diamond, didn't she?" my wife said, for Burton had just given Liz the world's largest diamond. I reminded her of the story of the world's second largest – the Plotnik diamond. It was owned by Mrs Plotnik from Brooklyn, a middle-aged woman who always looked depressed. Someone once asked her why.

"Because it comes with a coyse," she said.

"What curse?"

"Mr Plotnik," she replied.

Long after this, when Burton had been dead for eight years, and Liz was on her seventh husband, I was back in Dublin for one of an increasing number of family funerals. Browsing in a second-hand bookshop in Baggot Street, I came across a copy of *One Doctor in His Time*, Bethel Solomons's autobiography, published in 1956. There were some fascinating photographs in the book, of his bust by Epstein, of his meeting De Valera, and of the Irish rugby team of 1908, with B Solomons seated on the end of the middle row, a large man among some even larger men.

I bought the book to find out more about Burton's "real

The Irish XV, 1908. Bethel Solomons seated middle row end on right.

Jew". Privileged would have been a more accurate word than "real". His family were wealthy and educated English Jews who had settled in Dublin in the 1860s for business reasons. When Bethel was born there in 1885, most of Ireland's future Jews were still in Lithuania. What he describes of his early years is a strange mix of typical Edwardian Anglo-Irish family life and observant Judaism. He omits to mention that the Jewish population of Dublin multiplied nearly ten-fold in the first fifteen years of his life, from 283 in the 1881 census to 2,048 in the 1901 census.

Bethel was born into the aristocracy of Dublin Jewry, his mother a noted philanthropist and social worker. She and her husband helped found the Adelaide Road synagogue and religious school, where she taught for many years. It was this same cod-Romanesque synagogue that had brought together this disparate community of wealthy Anglicised Jews and the new, highly orthodox immigrants, and it was all done in less than a generation.

Though no literary masterpiece, *One Doctor in His Time* has incidental pleasures and surprises. It illustrates how much easier it was to be a Renaissance man in the earlier part of the twentieth century. Already a doctor, and having played rugby for three years for Ireland, Bethel Solomons indulged his passion for the stage by landing the leading role, under the name Thomas Thornhill, at the Abbey in Strindberg's *There are Crimes and Crimes*, directed by the great Lennox Robinson. Despite good reviews, he got the acting bug out of his system and returned to medicine. Thirteen years later he was Master of the Rotunda. A man of such talent and confidence would clearly have no trouble in taking on the Irish medical establishment, which, like most medical hierarchies, combined arrogance and egocentricity in equal measure. Judging by his book, a little of this mixture inevitably rubbed off on Bethel Solomons himself. Written when he was seventy, the book charts his highly successful career, and what he chooses to expose of his private life and attitudes has a splendidly Edwardian ring.

His marriage, like so many in Ireland, was undertaken at a mature age. In relation to his children and property he uses "my" and "mine" rather than "our". His "Seven rules for married happiness" advised: "Don't have in-laws to live with you. Don't have petty quarrels that lead to big ones. Don't read each other's letters. Children are the cement of matrimony, so decide on them beforehand. The wife should run the domestic side of the house, and never bother the husband with servant talk." And, finally, the simple admonition : "Continue to love one other."

On the subject of homosexuality, he is equally forthright. Solomons believed it could be a congenital, or an acquired, characteristic. If not the former, firm steps should be taken to avoid the latter. Every boy should be taught to box before being sent off to a Public School. He personally taught his two sons before he packed them off. After a month he received a letter from his eldest:

> Dear Father
>
> Thanks very much for teaching me to box and telling me about boys messing about. I had an experience of this kind with a boy who is two years older. I fought with him and knocked him unconscious ...

"I was a very proud father when I got this note," Solomons wrote in his autobiography, "and am glad to say that both sons are now married to delightful girls." Both sons, Bethel and Michael, went on to become highly successful consultants.

As for religion, Bethel Solomons grew increasingly impatient with orthodox Judaism, finding its practices sterile and archaic. "My emotional loyalty to the Jewish people is primarily racial," he wrote, "rather than religious or political." He flirted with the Unitarians, but when he learned the full horror of Nazi policies towards the Jews, he came back to the fold, or at least a fold, becoming a founder member of Dublin's Liberal Synagogue, and then its President. Well into his sixties, he alternated his Sabbaths between synagogue services and riding with the North Kildare Hunt.

After finishing *One Doctor in His Time*, I reflected on that one meeting my father and I had with the great man on St Stephen's Green. I was too young then to realise that he had been my father's role model. There were a hundred reasons why my father himself could never be a Bethel Solomons, but I'm sure he thought I could be. And that aspiration was to become one of the problems between us.

9. End of an Emergency

My father was right about one thing – the War wasn't over yet, and Hitler did have something up his sleeve. In fact, he had two things – the V-1 and the V-2. In London there was a lull between the end of the Blitz and the start of the Flying Bomb campaign. My mother and brother were back in London, and I had come back to be with them for the school holidays. My arrival coincided with that of the V-1s', or Doodlebugs, which seemed such a cute, Walt Disney name for such terrifying contraptions. Small, black, and unmanned, they looked, according to a Cockney commentator, "as though their arses were on fire", an effect caused by the burning jet-fuel expelled through their tail. Their engine made a stuttering noise, and when it finally cut out, one supposedly had only ten seconds before it crashed and exploded.

My father had already arranged our trip back to Dublin, but not before we heard our first Doodlebug in the night. Its stuttering engine grew louder, and then, overhead, it cut out. I heard my mother and brother rushing downstairs. My father shouted to me. I lay rigid in bed, terrified. Starting to count had been a mistake – the first time I was actually aware of the possibility of death. One could start counting up to ten, but one might not get beyond nine. I was up to five when my father rushed into the room. I thought he was going to shout at me, but suddenly he seemed paralysed too. Later I realised that we were both claustrophobic and would rather have been blown up on the first floor than buried alive downstairs. My mother shouted for us to come down. At eight I began praying to myself. I remember it because it was the first time I had ever prayed in fear, and I prayed in Hebrew. At ten there was still a silence – followed a few seconds later by an almighty crump. The house shook for an instant, but the Flying Bomb must have landed some way off as no windows were broken. Lying there, I wondered how many people had been blown to bits somewhere up the road.

And that was it – till the next day. It was a Sunday and my father and I were out cycling along the River Lea, the nearest countryside to Hackney. The road was deserted. A single-decker bus overtook us just as we heard the Doodlebug. It was coming straight at us, low and fast. My father shouted something. I didn't hear what it was. I simply imitated him. For a portly man, he moved with amazing agility. In one flowing movement he threw himself off his bike and into a ditch. The Doodlebug was almost overhead. The descriptions had done it justice. It was small, black, and sinister, its engine noise uneven and asthmatic, and its arse was indeed on fire. The bus stopped. The driver and his passengers poured out and threw themselves into the ditch a few yards up from where we lay. The Doodlebug was by now overhead. We all put our arms protectively over our heads as we had seen people do in films.

The stuttery engine however didn't cut out, and this particular Doodlebug kept going, and going, and going. Lowering our arms, we watched it heading for the horizon. It disappeared, and we never even heard the explosion. Slowly and self-consciously we all got up from the ditch and began to brush ourselves down. We looked at each other sheepishly, and several people giggled. After all we were British, and we had rather made asses of ourselves. But just before we got back on our bikes I looked at my father. There was hatred on his face as he looked after the Doodlebug and said *"In drerd zollen ze verin!"* I remember the words quite clearly because my father never swore in front of us. But I knew it meant – "May they rot in hell!" I wonder had he said it in Yiddish because it helped him identify with his fellow-Jews? He obviously knew what was happening to them not so far away on the Continent. Next day my mother, brother, and I were back on the route I seemed to have been travelling since shortly after I was born – the train from Euston to Holyhead, followed by the boat from Holyhead to Dun Laoghaire. My father stayed behind to minister to the sick and the Doodlebugged of Hackney. And I went back to school in Dublin feeling like a war hero.

I was brought up to believe that our families, both Prices and Whites, had been historically and geographically fortunate, blessed with a sort of cosmic good luck. In choosing Ireland, my grandparents had enabled their families to sidestep the worst horrors of the century: the pogroms, two World Wars, and the Holocaust. Keeping out of the way of the Black and Tans, or hearing an IRA man overhead on the roof, was a small price to pay for our survival. Years later, on my first visit to Jerusalem, I went to visit the tomb of David in its tower on the old wall. After paying the entrance fee, I was immediately accosted by a young *chassid* collecting money for his ultra-orthodox sect. He offered something in exchange. He had permission to say *kaddish* in this holy place and would say it for any of my family killed in the Holocaust, if I provided the Hebrew name. I told him that my family had lost no one. He stared back at me incredulously. Was it possible there was a European Jew who had lost no one in the *Shoah*? The odds were entirely against it. He then realised I was English and changed his tack. He would say *kaddish* for a loved one lost fighting the Nazis. I had lost no one that way either, and I briefly experienced "survivors' guilt". Moreover it would have taken too long to explain to him how we had escaped unscathed. Instead I remembered my Uncle Marks's eighteen months as a doctor in the Flying Corps in World War I. At least he had fought against the Kaiser, even though he had died in bed. I handed over the money, and my *chassid* went off to say *kaddish* for the soul of *Moshe ben Bezalel Dov*.

Marks and my father had been the only Prices to come and live in England, yet they were too old to serve in the armed forces in World War II. The only family combatant had been my daredevil Uncle Arthur, my mother's brother, who had possessed one of the first private pilot's licenses in Ireland in the 1930s. When he heard what Hitler was doing to the Jews on the Continent, he vowed to kill him. His chosen method was the bomb, and he would personally drop it. With this goal in mind, he came to England and volunteered for the RAF. Aged thirty-nine, he was too old for flight crew, but he faked his age and became a bomber navigator. He was not going to trust anybody else to get the plane directly over the Reichstag or Berchesgarten. He flew several missions over Germany, but sadly for the world, never succeeded in his real objective. Then, in 1943, he had some sort of breakdown, for which he received treatment from a Harley Street psychiatrist attached to the RAF. By war's end Arthur was invalided out – and living with the psychiatrist in a fine stately home in Somerset. Together they looked after a handful of rich, semi-permanent psychiatric patients in one wing of the house. The psychiatrist was married, but there was some mystery as to where his wife fitted into this picture.

I once overheard a heated argument between my mother and her sister-in-law, Miriam, wife of my Uncle Michael who had negotiated with me through the locked bathroom door. Miriam's tone with my mother was clearly patronising. "Oh, come on, Gypsy, don't be so dim. You don't think he's still Arthur's psychiatrist, do you? They live together, for God's sake. They're homosexual."

There was a momentary silence, and then my mother let fly, her Irish brogue broadening as it always did when she was angry.

"What rubbish! What wicked nonsense! How dare you? Don't you dare talk like that in my house."

My mother was perfectly clear about one thing – no brother

of hers could possibly be a homosexual. Occasionally Arthur visited our house with his psychiatrist friend, who was the epitome of a very English Harley Street consultant. In my mother's admiring eyes, he was obviously even less of a homosexual than her brother. For her, homosexuals were ballet dancers and interior decorators – almost certainly not English, definitely not Irish, and never, never Jewish. It was only late in life that she realised that some ballet dancers and decorators were heterosexual, and a lot of other men, some of them Irish or even Jewish, weren't. I was amazed how, in her seventies, she accepted such shocks with equanimity. For her generation, this gradual acceptance of difference was one of the few beneficial effects of television. By then, however, Arthur and his friend were dead.

In the last year of the War, Hitler sent over his last secret weapon – the V-2 rocket. It was the beginning of missile warfare, a threat that has haunted the world ever since. The V-2s arrived silent and unseen. As with the V-1, hearing the explosion meant that you had survived it. One thousand and fifty V-2s fell on Southern England, mostly on London, and killed upwards of 30,000 people. My mother, Ashley, and I returned to London in time to hear several of the last explosions, fortunately distant. With the War nearly over, my father had decided that it was time for us to be a united family again and take our place once more in the Irish-Jewish Diaspora.

To my dismay, I had been withdrawn from Wesley at the end of a term. I took a written test for a London day school and did rather poorly. I was then interviewed by a solemn English headmaster who said that he was prepared to make allowances for my much-interrupted education. He told me that I would have to get used to playing soccer, not rugby. This news was anathema to me, putting paid to my ambition to score the winning Irish try against England. I must have reacted miserably, for he tried to relax proceedings by getting me to

113

speak some Gaelic to him. My dreams of Lansdowne Road receding, I mumbled a few surly sentences.

It would have been small comfort for me at the time to know that I was in good company, one of tens of thousands of boys and girls returning to their original homes from evacuation to the country or further afield. Some I met later had been with relatives in America, Canada, or Australia and had not seen either of their parents, or siblings, for nearly six years. Readjustment was painful all round and frequently created permanent family problems. My problem was that I had had too good a war and had grown used to playing a pivotal role in a one-parent family. Indeed I had become almost a paterfamilias, having learned to cope with my mother's uneven discipline and her bouts of anger. Much of my speed and penetration on the rugby field came from the instant momentum acquired when I saw her reach for any stick or broom that came to hand. When it came to discipline and religious observance, however, my father had higher, more consistent standards.

Much later I came to realise that the Ireland I knew as a boy, and subsequently missed enormously, bore little relation to the realities of life for the mass of Irish people at the time. For me there were always three Irelands, the one my parents and their friends waxed so nostalgic about, the one I had experienced personally, and the one that belonged to the vast Catholic majority, and from which they emigrated in droves. As Evelyn Waugh said, "To the Irishman there are only two final realities, hell and the United States." With the post-War tightening of American immigration laws, Waugh's remark must be amended, substituting the UK for the US. Between 1946 and 1961, over half-a-million Irish emigrated to Britain, reducing the domestic population to 2.8 million.

With so many Irish coming to England, I was in a tiny minority wanting to head in the opposite direction. At the time, however, I was politically and economically naive, unaware of the drawbacks of de Valera's Ireland. His isolationist and nationalist policies may have brought peace and a sense of independent identity, but at the cost of creating a cloistered and economically backward society.

I have a memory of being made to sit and listen to one of de Valera's St Patrick's Day broadcasts. I have no memory of what he said, just of his rather lugubrious voice. It might even have been the famous 1943 broadcast when he had lauded the Gaelic revival, and talked of a culture where "in the countryside young men and women danced at the crossroads". He obviously did not envisage much traffic outside of Dublin. He went on to talk of "a people who were satisfied by frugal comfort and devoted their leisure to things of the spirit". These austere spiritual and cultural aspirations were clearly not shared by the large number of emigrating Irish. And enjoying myself in Rathgar and Sandycove, I too knew nothing of them.

An earlier exile, James Joyce, whose last visit home was in 1912, wrote of a country where "Christ and Caesar were hand in glove". As my father and his friends discovered, the overpowering influence of the Catholic Church in all social and educational matters extended to medical ethics and practice as well. Despite the odd exceptions, like the Solomons and Abrahamson families, the odds were heavily stacked against a non-Catholic doctor being selected, never mind promoted, by predominantly Catholic hospital boards. Apart from the obvious taboos on abortion, birth-control, and divorce, there was always the suspicion that a non-Catholic doctor might hold liberal and heretical views on sexual practice, the size of families, or the rights of women. Thus unable to find suitable hospital work, my father and his Irish-Jewish medical colleagues left to find work in Britain. Their only alternative would have been to stay and go into general practice. To do this they would have needed premises on which to put up their plates, and sufficient financial resources to sit it out while they built up a practice. Few of the Jewish graduates of my father's generation had had the wherewithal for this approach. Many of them had worked their way through college, or had parents who had scrimped and saved to send them there. The majority of them had gone to the Royal College of Surgeons, rather than the more expensive and socially exclusive Trinity.

Nor was Ireland the welcoming country it had once been. Ironically, for a country with such massive emigration, tighter immigration laws were introduced in the late 1930s, just as the Nazi threat to European Jewry was first being realised. At an international conference at Evian in 1938, attempts were made to raise immigration quotas, but Ireland, like most other countries, rejected any change. On exhibition at the Irish-Jewish Museum in Dublin is a letter, dated 9th October, 1938, from Isaac Herzog, who had moved from Dublin to become Chief Rabbi of Palestine:

> Dear Mr de Valera,
> I am appealing to you to admit a quota of Jewish refugee doctors and dentists to practice in Eire on the same conditions as in the United Kingdom.
> A considerable number have been admitted into England and allowed to set up practices ...

The letter goes on to enumerate conditions and suggest some very minimal figures. After a brief exchange of letters the request was refused. In the following year, the leading members of the Irish-Jewish community wrote to the Minister for Home Affairs requesting some limited sanctuary for persecuted Jews on the Continent. They pointed out how considerable money from British and Continental sources, much of it from the Rothchilds, had been donated to help the Irish during the Great Famine. The appeal again fell on deaf ears. There is no way of knowing whether this decision was due to general xenophobia, or specific anti-Semitism.

There had always been a strand of reactionary Catholic anti-Semitism in Ireland. It was not only the long shadow that Father Creagh cast from Limerick; rather its roots went back, via Rome, to that much earlier, seminal event in Jerusalem. It was the traditional Christian anti-Semitism of the You-Crucified-Our-Lord variety. The best answer to this charge came from the late and great American comedian Lenny Bruce, who countered such accusations at school with "It wasn't me. I swear it. It was Uncle Maxie. There's a letter from him in the attic, admitting everything – 'It was me, Uncle Maxie. I did it!'"

In the 1930s the dismissed Police Commissioner, General Eoin O'Duffy, formed his Fascist Blueshirt movement, modelled on the Blackshirts and Brownshirts of Germany and Italy and Mosley's Fascists nearer home. Members were recruited mainly from disgruntled ex-IRA and Army men. Greenshirts might have seemed more appropriate in Ireland, but it was said that O'Duffy bought a job lot of blue shirts from a Jewish manufacturer, without divulging the purpose for which they were to be used. The Blueshirts operated briefly on the fringes of a coalition opposition party. Like other right-wing and anti-Semitic groups in Ireland their activities were mercifully short-lived. O'Duffy himself went off to lead a pro-Franco Irish Brigade in the Spanish Civil War, survived, and was given a state funeral in 1944. A year earlier, there was another brief manifestation of this especial prejudice in a Dáil debate when a celebrated bigot, Oliver Flanagan, proposed emergency orders:

> ... directed against the Jews, who crucified our Saviour nineteen hundred years ago and who are crucifying us every day of the week ... There is one thing that Germany did, and this was to rout the Jews out of their country. Until we rout the Jews out of this country, it does not matter what orders you make.

There were at this time only 5,000 Jews in the whole of Ireland, including myself. I never saw one of them, not even Uncle Maxie, trying to crucify a Christian. Flanagan supplied no further details, but then paranoia disdains proof. At least his proposal was laughed out of the Dáil.

In the same year the Longford County Council unanimously passed a resolution:

> ... that the attention of the government be directed to the fact that several foreigners, mainly Jews, have succeeded in having their names changed to names of Irish origin, and that the Longford County Council protest against this practice being permitted to continue in the interest of the community, and that copies of this resolution be sent to each county council in Eire.

While the Irish government did nothing about this, it did circulate the protest to the other county councils. The only other council to adopt the resolution was County Tipperary, so maybe it's a good thing that "it's a long way to Tipperary".

Later that year de Valera received a letter, still in the National Archive, which was postmarked Rathgar and signed "Brian Boru (late Abraham Goldstein)". It enclosed a clipping from *The Gazette* of 21st May, 1943, under the heading "Change of Name":

> COHEN, Louis Jacob to Louis Jacob Collins, of 35, Rathdown Park, Terenure. Parents: COHEN, Norman and Rachel, to Norman Collins and Rachel Collins.

The accompanying letter stated that:

> Notices similar to the enclosed have become very frequent lately in *The Gazette*. Already I know of O'Brien, O'Sullivan (late Solomon), Sheridan, Byrne etc., and now we have Collins. At this rate the Irish people will very soon be known by their characteristic noses and olive complexions, not to mention their thieving propensities. Do you not think the time has come to give up the study of

Irish and replace it in the schools by Yiddish, as undoubtedly the latter is going to become the language that matters in Ireland?

There is no record of Dev replying to Brian Boru, né Goldstein.

There was no question of de Valera personally being anti-Semitic. My father, like a million other expatriates, called him Dev, admired him, and paid him the ultimate compliment by saying "Dev's yer man". Whenever the British government took issue with the Irish, my father would say, "Don't worry. Dev's well able for them." Given my father's own religious devotion, he could only respect de Valera's staunch Catholicism. Dev's austere and non-materialist views also struck a sympathetic chord with my father. After all, hadn't my father's own wife and children been bodily spoilt and spiritually starved by the materialistic life of his in-laws in Rathgar and Sandycove? The secret of the relationship between my father and Dev was that Dev was a Catholic Puritan and my father a Jewish one. They were brothers under the skin.

There were, however, some aspects of de Valera's policies that I never quite understood my father accepting. For example, my father hated the Germans, yet seemed quite comfortable with de Valera's rigid neutrality. Possibly his acquiescence was based more on personal considerations than principle, given that Irish neutrality offered his family a haven. We were safe there in Dublin, with the Irish Sea in place, and there was the additional advantage that his three sisters would never risk the German submarines to come and visit him in England. When Hitler died in 1945, just as the full horror of the concentration camps was becoming known, de Valera went personally to the German Embassy in Dublin to express his formal condolences. The British Consul explained it as "Neutrality observed with mathematical consistency". Not for nothing had de Valera originally been a maths teacher. Despite this gesture, when Dev became President in 1959 my father's admiration for him continued unabated. In the end I think Dev and Ireland existed in a special corner of his mind, a sort of free port where the normal customs and tariffs didn't apply.

10. Aftermaths

If our families had avoided casualties during the War, we were not so fortunate in the peace. It was as if our ration of woes had been carefully stored away for the duration to be unpacked now. The first casualty of the peace was my Auntie Polly. My parents never discussed serious family matters in front of their children. What we knew was pieced together from quick asides or one-sided phone conversations. My understanding of my Auntie Polly was that she was very difficult rather than very ill. Her condition, whatever it was, had apparently been exacerbated by being blown out of bed by that German bomb four years before. Warned that she was coming to stay with us, I eavesdropped on my father soothing my agitated mother and gathered that Polly was not the vanguard of an entire spinster-aunt invasion. Rather she had been causing acute disharmony among her sisters. They were all now in their forties. Suitable suitors or profitable employment had failed to materialise and they still lived on the South Circular Road looking after their bed-ridden mother.

Polly duly arrived in London. I gathered that she was here for some sort of medical examination. Extremely short-sighted, she had those highly magnifying lenses that made it look as though her eyes were painted on the back of her glasses. Always rather large with a fine tracery of dark facial hair, she was now fatter, and there was more dark hair than usual sprouting on her chin. I hoped I wouldn't be expected to kiss her, but there was no escape. If not the prettiest of the sisters, I remembered her at least as the jolliest. But now she was quiet and preoccupied, and her arrival spread a pall over the house. Then, one afternoon, a few days after she arrived, she came out of her bedroom onto the landing and started to scream. Her mouth was open very wide, and the scream poured out of it, high, sharp, and seemingly endless.

My parents ran to her and tried unsuccessfully to calm her down. The screaming continued, turning into a low growl while she took breath. Ashley and I watched horrified from the stairs. My mother, near hysterics herself, kept shouting at my father, "Do something. Do something. You're a doctor." Then, her hands over her ears, she ran into her bedroom and shut the door, leaving my father to try and stop that unrelenting noise. Seeing us watching at the stairs, he rushed down and pressed a ten-shilling note into my hand. Gesturing at Ashley, who was about six at the time, he said, "Take him to the pictures – quickly." I looked up at the landing. Polly was staring down at us, the huge, magnified eyes, the mouth wide-open, the scream coming out of it straight at us. Clutching the money in one hand, and Ashley's hand in the other, I turned and ran out of the house.

We went to the Regent, Stamford Hill, but I don't remember what "picture" we saw. We dreaded going home, but when we arrived back Polly had gone. My parents looked shattered, and my father said Polly was very unwell and had gone to a hospital. Nothing further was explained. I never saw Polly again. Later I learned that she went initially to a private psychiatric clinic. At first my father and Marks footed the bill. They were also still helping support their mother and other two sisters in Dublin, a not uncommon situation for expatriate Irish males with spinster sisters. The nearest census to this period, in 1941, showed that twenty per cent of women over forty-five in Ireland were unmarried.

As Polly's condition showed no signs of improvement, she looked set to become a heavy long-term drain on the family's finances. My father now sought the help of his de facto brother-in-law, Arthur's psychiatrist friend. As the National Health Service had just been introduced, with my father's full approval, he now tried personally to benefit from it, and Arthur's friend managed to get Polly into a Health Service psychiatric hospital. The only diagnosis ever mentioned was that she had "a hysterical condition". Her medical records have long since vanished, but most likely she was diagnosed as a schizophrenic. In those days combined drug and psychotherapy treatment for severe conditions was in an early stage of development. Acute cases of depression, anxiety, or obsessional disorders, and occasionally schizophrenia, were treated surgically with a frontal leucotomy, which became more generally known as a lobotomy. This procedure, as described in the *Oxford Textbook of Psychiatry* (2nd edition, 1989), entails "extensive cutting in the white matter of the frontal lobes made through lateral burr holes."

It was a not uncommon operation between the 1940s and the 1960s. The same textbook notes that after initial improvement in patients there followed adverse side-effects, "including intellectual impairment, emotional lability, disinhibition, apathy, incontinence, obesity and epilepsy." If ever there was a case of the cure being worse than the disease, surely this was it. By the 1970s the incidence of such operations was drastically reduced. Small-scale follow-up studies showed some success in very depressed and highly anxious patients after leucotomies, but virtually none with schizophrenics, only the adverse side effects.

At the time my father had little knowledge of psychiatric practice, but I don't think he ever forgave himself for allowing this operation to be performed on his sister. However, if he needed to expiate his guilt the means were on hand. After the operation Polly was transferred to the NHS psychiatric hospital and sanitorium at Virginia Water in Surrey. It was a horrendous drive there from North London, before the advent of ring roads and motorways, yet my father visited her as often as possible. At first it was every fortnight, and my mother would go with him. Sometimes Polly recognised them, sometimes she didn't. Despite the operation she could still become abusive, as occasionally happened when they took her out to tea in the sedate tea shoppes of nearby Weybridge or Windsor.

When I was fourteen or so, my mother told me about one such scene. It gave me my first insight into why farce and tragedy are such close neighbours. The scene, as she described it, stayed vividly in my mind. There they were, my Irish-Jewish parents, squashed into a corner table, already feeling out-of-place in the heartland of the Anglican stockbroker belt, a stone's throw from the Royal Family itself. Suddenly the short-sighted, hugely fat, bearded woman in their company starts hurling abuse at the refined toasted-teacake eaters around them. Given the infinite English capacity for looking the other way when faced with social embarrassment, the most tremendous staring out of windows and searching in handbags must have ensued, while my father coaxed his sister out into the street, and my mother paid for the uneaten cucumber sandwiches and the half-drunk tea.

My father invariably came home from these trips with a migraine and retired to bed. After a while, my mother could bear it no longer and urged my father not to go. She gave them up, but he persisted. I dreaded that one day he would ask me to go with him, but he never did, and I, cowardly and ingrate son, never volunteered. Instead he usually found some long-suffering second cousin, or London-Irish-Jewish doctor friend to keep him company, as he drove backwards and forwards to Virginia Water every fortnight or so for twenty-six years.

Polly, in a mostly vegetable state, outlived my father by ten years. After he died, the power of attorney for Polly passed to me. The duties were not onerous, mainly a matter of receiving her tiny pension, sending most of it to the hospital authorities for any necessary clothing, and sending any remainder to the two sisters left in Dublin. At this point I had also become the recipient of the letters previously sent to my father each week on the eve of the Sabbath. Mercifully mine came fortnightly. Along with hints about the terrible cost of living in Dublin, they kept asking if I was visiting Polly. Still physically and psychologically squeamish, I had not seen Auntie Polly in those twenty-six years. Had I visited, it was most unlikely she would have known who I was. I wrote this rationale back to the aunts. Their next letter again asked if I had visited Polly. I gave up trying to explain anything to them. Concerned that Polly herself might wonder where my father was, I phoned the hospital and asked the matron if she could break the news. She called back a few days later to say Polly had taken the news with no more than passing interest. In fact, she never referred to her brother again. It was as though his long years of penance on the A30 and the A315 had gone for naught.

Ten years later the same matron phoned to tell me that Polly had died peacefully at eighty, having spent the last half of her life not knowing up from down. Another funeral at Bushey had to be arranged. It proved a replay of my father's. The Girls had to be flown over from Dublin and met at the airport. Once again my mother observed that they would look as if they had come off the Ark, and indeed they did. Only this time their clothes were ten years older. Once again we sat *shiva* in my parents' flat, my mother, brother, Aunts Minnie and Hilda, and myself sitting on low stools. This time we did it for only three days, rather than the full week. Few people joined us in our mourning. Hardly anyone remembered Polly, and four of the five principal mourners had not seen her for forty years.

At some point, years before Polly died, I went to an exhibition in London and saw for the first time Edvard Munch's *The Scream*. His woman was thin and the scene outdoors, but her eyes were staring out of their sockets, her mouth was stretched wide-open, and I could feel the noise pouring out. Suddenly I was back in our house in Clapton, and Polly was on the landing, screaming down at us.

My father's brother, my Uncle Marks, did not get to figure much in this family tragedy. Shortly after Polly was permanently hospitalised, Marks decided that he should go to Dublin, see his mother and sisters, and try to explain things to them. As I was on holiday from my London day-school, and longed to go back to Dublin, he took me with him. We shared his supply of Fox's Glacier Mints on that much-travelled route from Euston to Holyhead to Dun Laoghaire, and I vowed to myself that one day I would smoke a pipe just as he did, drive a Riley with a long bonnet, and probably stay a bachelor. I only discovered much later about his relationship with a rich, non-Jewish widow, an ex-patient. Marks was fairly observant, and the taboo of marrying-out must have weighed heavily on him.

I stayed with my maternal grandmother in Rathgar, while Marks stayed in the house on the South Circular Road in the bedroom so recently vacated by Polly. He had a pain in his leg that had started on the boat coming over. Thinking it was rheumatic, he sent me out to the chemist with his prescription for some tablets. In fact he had a thrombosis, and three days later he was dead. His body was carried out past the bedroom door of my bed-ridden Grandma Price, who had lost a son and, to all intents and purposes, a daughter within a few months of each other.

My parents came to Dublin for the funeral. We stayed together in the White House, which now seemed sad and empty. My Grandmother, who was going increasingly blind, lived there with a maid and a part-time gardener who could drive – but very dangerously. I gathered from muttered family conversations that her income was rapidly dwindling, and that the gardener, whom she was very fond of, would likely quite literally drive her to her death. After sitting *shiva* in the even sadder house on the South Circular Road, we went back to London. My father came home to perform the obligatory month of mourning required for a sibling. He went to synagogue every morning to say *kaddish* and stayed away from the cinema, theatre, concerts, or any social festivities. Before the end of that same year, his mother died. He went to the funeral in Dublin, and sat *shiva* again for a week, before coming home to observe the full year of mourning required for a parent. It was like full Court mourning in Victorian times, except for the daily trips to synagogue. It made no difference that he had just done all this for his brother. In Orthodox Judaism there is no remission for good mourning.

It must have been particularly grim to be in mourning at a time when everybody else was celebrating the peace. I am sure he kept to the rigid rules of his orthodoxy because he truly believed in them and gained comfort from the routines and camaraderie of the early morning services. Nor did he miss the cultural deprivations as much as my mother. She loved the theatre, cinema, dancing, and the bright lights generally. However, the deaths were not in her family, and after a few months my father turned a blind eye if my mother went out with friends to various entertainments. The rule seemed to be that she should never talk about it afterwards. It might have been almost understandable had my mother taken a lover, or at least a presentable male escort. This, however, given their observant, orthodox middle-classness, was about as likely as my father converting to Catholicism. In such a traumatic time, as my father raced twice daily between surgery and synagogue, an eldest son should have been a source of support and comfort. Instead I was exactly the opposite, a confused adolescent, confused about nationality, religion, and sex. In those days there wasn't a lot else to be confused about. The "Bolshie" my father remembered on his deathbed was born here.

With the War over, I was back in London. While I had just had my barmitzvah and was, in religious terms, a man, I didn't feel like one, and certainly wasn't treated like one. No doubt in biblical times, boys became men in the hot climate of the Holy

Land before you could say "Leviticus and Deuteronomy". In chilly, post-War North London no one seemed prepared to recognise my manhood at thirteen. In the couple of years preceding barmitzvah, I had been bombarded, like all orthodox Jewish youth, with lessons in Hebrew and religious knowledge. In the synagogue, on the appointed Sabbath, standing on the reader's dais, uncomfortable in a new suit and black shoes that pinched, I had chanted in rabbinical plainsong a long portion of the Torah. Afterwards there was the traditional party, where the self-conscious barmitzvah boy made a ritual speech fulsomely thanking all the people whose great sacrifices had made possible his fine upbringing. I later realised it was the prototype of the Oscar-acceptance speech – "I would first like to thank God, my parents, all my grandparents, uncles and aunts, my agent, the producers and director of this wonderful bar-mitzvah …" – only differing at the very end, when one promises to be a good and observant Jew for the rest of one's life. It is a promise that around eighty per cent of Jews will inevitably break before many Yom Kippurs have come and gone. Like lapsed Catholics, all they have committed themselves to is a life-long guilty conscience.

The only advantage this new status appeared to confer was my being eligible to count towards a *minyan*, the ten men required for any religious service. Given my low boredom threshold and the length of the services, it was a dubious privilege. There were newly acquired duties too. One of the most irksome was putting on *tefillim*, those two little boxes and their accompanying leather thongs with which my paternal grandfather had seemingly taken his own blood pressure in hospital. I had to wear them with a prayer shawl to say morning prayers at home. It meant on weekdays getting up twenty minutes earlier. There were also no more excuses allowed for not going to synagogue on Saturday morning and staying for the whole service, a period of up to three hours, depending on the length of the sermon. Full synagogue attendance was likewise required for all major religious holidays, as was fasting for the entire twenty-five hours of the Day of Atonement.

It was in those first years of peace abroad that war broke out at home. Still in mourning for Wesley, where I'd even enjoyed the Gaelic lessons, I now attended Mercers, one of those London day schools originally founded by a trade guild, and now a Holborn office block. After my time in the Irish system, I was not so much behind my class as at a tangent to it. Once in a maths class, after I had given a totally wrong answer, the Master said, "Perhaps Irish geometry is different, Price." I was too humiliated to mention that the Irish still called it Euclid.

Having already communed in Hebrew with the Jewish God for twenty minutes before leaving home, I was in no mood to go through it all over again for the Christian God when I got to school. Here at least the Jews were allowed to stay in the hall for prayers, not kept in an adjoining room to race in like trained ferrets in time for announcements. It was a relief to be able to sing hymns and pray in English, but whenever it came to "through Jesus Christ, our Lord" or "Father, Son and Holy Ghost", we clamped our mouths firmly shut. We were the ones who would go up to Heaven. The others, who had backed the wrong saviour, the Trinity instead of the Unity, would go in the opposite direction. These superior thoughts lasted only a very short time.

The greatest horror, however, was reserved for Tuesday and Thursday afternoons. Since Mercers played soccer, it was now certain that I would never run on in green at Lansdowne Road, a shamrock over my heart. I adjusted begrudgingly to the round ball, understanding totally how Webb Ellis felt on that memorable day at Rugby School when he picked up the ball and ran. However, because I was fast I was selected for a junior school team, after which all hell broke out at home.

School matches were played on a Saturday, and my father said that I couldn't play. Playing meant not only missing synagogue, but travelling on the Sabbath. I wasn't keen on soccer, but even a choice even between soccer and synagogue was no contest. The big rows happened at the dinner table. As I expressed strong anti-Sabbatarian sentiments, his face would suddenly go white with anger. It never went red, or white via red, but straight from normal pink to bloodless white. One of his hands scratched furiously at the palm of the other, as he shouted "Say one more word and you'll go flying away from this table." He was to use that expression frequently over the next couple of years. Invariably about religion, the arguments proceeded with chess-like logic to their climax – my assisted flight.

Initially I looked to my mother for help. After all, she had let me play rugby on Saturdays in Dublin. No help was forthcoming. A veil had been drawn over those days. Instead, aware my father and I were on a collision course, she would give me a series of warning looks and head-shakings. When I ignored them, she directed this mime equally unsuccessfully at my father, while I continued to disagree furiously with him about what God required of us. Ashley, aged six or so, sat like an anxious spectator at a tennis match. Eventually my father went into white-face and issued his threat. He never actually hit me, but his anger reduced me to silence. For years his threat haunted me. It took on a sort of cartoon reality, like a sequence from Tom and Jerry – that one day my father would actually lean across and strike with enough velocity for me to "fly away from the table". With this one paternal blow, I would achieve lift-off. Arms outstretched, I would circle the room before, to their consternation, banking gracefully out of the door and swooping up the stairs and into my bedroom. There, gliding over bed and desk and out through the open window, I would be off, Mary Poppins-like, over the rooftops. Then it was up, up, and away, climbing steadily over Stamford Hill, Wood Green, and Watford, setting a course north by northwest till seeing the glint of the Irish Sea, the welcoming, outstretched breakwaters of Dun Laoghaire harbour, I finally swooped down on Dublin, arms tired but spirits high. I always had a good sense of direction, walking or flying.

I refused to tell the school I couldn't play on Saturdays. If that was what my father wanted, then he could tell them himself. He was always reluctant to confront what he thought of as establishment authority, but after several more arguments he gave in and wrote a letter. I was excused all further Saturday fixtures. I occasionally played in a mid-week fixture, but it was effectively the end of my sporting career at Mercers. In their book I was nothing but a pallid, pasty-faced, weedy little Jew who put synagogue before soccer – at least that's what I thought they thought.

I was of course unaware at the time that I was merely part of a general social phenomenon that was afflicting my male peer group. With fathers away in the armed forces, boys, particularly the eldest or only son, had become the "man of the family". Furthermore, we had got used to the undivided attention of our mothers. You don't need a profound knowledge of Greek mythology or Viennese psychiatry to work out what complicated, if unwitting, emotions were engendered. Much as we were all no doubt happy to have our fathers back alive, a new authority figure was suddenly in residence, and a painful period of readjustment inevitably followed. In my own case the waters were further muddied by the religious differences.

In the 1930s the Jewish migration from the East End had been well underway. The Blitz, which destroyed much of the area, was the final spur to this exodus. Like their biblical ancestors leaving Egypt for the Promised Land, London Jews moved inexorably westward through Clapton and Stamford Hill to Hendon and Golders Green, and even on to greener Edgware and Stanmore. A sizeable Jewish middle-class now prospered in the major British cities, and they sought a good education for their children. The problem they confronted was what sort of education? There were no purely Jewish schools of any secular status, and most middle-class Jewish families wanted the cachet of sending their children to good English Public Schools. In the post-War period British Jews were intensely patriotic, having only been saved from the gas chambers by the Channel and Britain's refusal to surrender to the Nazis. In wanting the best of both worlds for their children, British and Jewish, it never occurred to them that there might be any conflict involved for their children. The psychiatric term "mixed messages" was still to be coined.

Still the messages arrived most mixedly. Many public schools, particularly London day schools, exercised Jewish quotas, usually of ten per cent. This practice created the unfortunate situation where clever Jewish boys competed against each other for the small number of places. "Too clever by half" is a favourite English put-down, but that is what a Jewish boy had to be to get into the school in the first place. Once in, Jewish boys had to conform to rules that usually insisted on chapel attendance, Saturday school or games, and taking off only a minimum of religious holidays. No even halfway-orthodox Jew could contemplate sending his children to such a school. The less orthodox, however, were willing to make compromises. Those who wouldn't, like my parents, found local grammar or direct-grant schools where their children could dodge between these two very different worlds.

At home one was expected to lead an observant, orthodox life. At school one did some things and not others. One ate one's own sandwiches rather than school lunches, was excused any activity that took place on Saturday or any religious holiday. For these lost days Jewish boys and girls had to catch up with schoolwork in their own time, presumably when their ambitious parents weren't trying to improve them further with music lessons, elocution lessons, extra maths tuition, ballet for girls, and Talmud for boys. It was a formidable routine – being cleverer, working harder, only eating kosher, going in and out of synagogue like a yo-yo, and, absolutely most important, written in words of fire, never ever looking at, let alone lusting after, a non-Jewish girl.

What was totally ignored in this whole schizophrenic process was the basic adolescent urge to conform to one's peer group while rebelling against the authority of the older generation. However the problem for our generation was which peer group – Jewish or Christian? Which authority – school or home? My choice was clear-cut. Home rule was the most irksome, and that was where my rebellion started. And my Lord North, my Louis XVI, was poor Mr Barnett.

Mr Barnett was my Hebrew teacher, as my father believed that my religious education should not stop with my barmitzvah. However, given my heavy schedule, a concession was granted. A teacher would come to the house instead of my spending Sunday mornings at synagogue classes. His duties would be to improve my classical Hebrew and history, and introduce me to the tautologies of the Talmud.

Mr Barnett was in his forties, a lean, energetic, hook-nosed man, with an insistent voice that whined in both English and Hebrew. Basically I liked him, except when he had one of his frequent colds. He had a large moustache that acted like a tea-strainer when he blew his nose. After this activity I couldn't bear to look at him for the rest of the lesson. He must have thought me shifty as well as heretical. But snotty moustache or not, I argued ceaselessly with him about almost any theological point he introduced.

Initially, I argued the standard rationalist line. Why, if God had created the world and all its peoples, did he favour the Jews and make them his Chosen People? For Mr Barnett that was easy. Jews were not chosen because they were better, but rather to spread His message and to set an example to other nations. Was it suprising then, I asked, if the other nations resented the Jews coming round with their message and presuming to set an example? After all, how do Jews themselves react when Jehovah's Witnesses knock on the door? "Tell them we're having dinner. Tell them we've got a religion already."

Mr Barnett tried to distract me with a biblical, Boys' Own, action-adventure story – the First Book of Samuel, in the original. That was a mistake too. It was 1946, we were all war-weary, and I sided totally with sad, put-upon Saul against God and Samuel, his smug prophet. To me the story was full of God's totally unwarranted and unfair interventions in Saul's life. Given this sort of God was it any wonder Saul had ended up as a history's first recorded case of manic-depression?

I also challenged Mr Barnett over Hebraic aggression. How did it set a good example to other nations if we went round smiting them, their women, children, and the asses within their gates? Wasn't that what the Nazis had done? That charge caused one of our major rows. Once he had calmed down and blown his nose through his moustache again, Mr Barnett said it was the way of the world in those times. Other nations had not accepted God's word. He asked if it was so different from what the Protestant Tudors and Catholic Stuarts had done? What about the Armada and the Spanish Inquisition? Wasn't that all about people acting out what they thought was God's command? To which I claimed, triumphantly, that all he was saying was how organised religion, belief in an exclusive God, led to bigotry and slaughter.

Our arguments used to run on long after the appointed hour. Apart from having his faith and patience sorely tested, poor Mr Barnett was losing money on the lessons. Yet I was at the wrong age, and it was the wrong time to be teaching this vengeful, divine interventionism. Adolescence was still an idealistic interlude. The war to end all wars had just been fought. We had only recently seen the newsreel pictures of Auschwitz and Belsen. Where was the interventionist God when six million of his Chosen People were being so horrendously smitten? It was not an easy time in which to be a good, old-fashioned, orthodox believer.

Still Mr Barnett kept his faith. He believed, as all orthodox Jews must, that the law was given directly by God to Moses on Mount Sinai, and there are some matters that it is not given to mere mortals to question. We agreed to disagree, and nonetheless he finally went to my father, saying I was an *apikoros*, and if he continued to teach me he might become one himself. According to Leo Rosten's *Joys of Yiddish* the word *apikoros* comes from the Greek philosopher Epicurus, via rabbinical literature. It means an unbeliever, a sceptic, an agnostic, an atheist. The *Mishnah* states, "All Israelites have a share in the future world, except he who says there is no resurrection, he who says the Law has not been given by God, and an *apikoros*." It seemed Mr Barnett and my share in the afterlife had disappeared simultaneously. However, I was soon to discover Spinoza and Pantheism instead.

Within a year of being at Mercers I had lost both my Irish accent and, according to my horrified parents, developed a Cockney whine. As well as a devout Jew, my parents wished me to become an English gentleman, or at least an Anglo-Irish-Jewish gentleman. And I wasn't going to become any of those things if I sounded like a Mile End costermonger. So I was packed off to an elocution teacher, a gaunt, middle-aged lady whose house, like her personality, lacked any warmth. In this icy atmosphere I practised flat vowel-sounds with a matchstick wedged upright between my front teeth. However, it must have paid off, as at the end of that year I won the Form elocution prize, any academic book of my choice. My book cost 8/6d (42½ pence) and was handsomely bound in green morocco and stamped with the school motto *Honor Deo*. It was called *Living Biographies of Great Philosophers* by Henry Thomas and Dana Lee Thomas, and I have it still. I always wondered whether they were husband and wife or brother and sister. Either way, I owe the Thomases a great deal. They arrived at just the right moment in my life.

Judging by their slightly over-the-top style, the Thomases

were American. Their opening paragraph on Spinoza begins:

> Spinoza's fate was unparalleled in the history of
> philosophy. As a rationalist he was severed from
> the Jews. As a Jew he was isolated from the world.
> Never was a man so lonely as Baruch Spinoza. Yet
> this loneliness was necessary for the development
> of his unique system of thought.

In my adolescent apostasy, here was a man after my own heart. Born in Amsterdam in 1632 of rich parents who wanted him to become a rabbi, Spinoza read Descartes at an early age and became a rationalist. Whereas I read Spinoza at an early age and became a pantheist. Or, to be more accurate, I tried to read Spinoza. The Thomases informed me that his most famous work *Ethics* was "originally composed in Latin, geometric in form, Greek in its idealism, based on the pantheism of the Italian Giordano Bruno, developed from the French mechanistic theories of Descartes, and Hebrew in its faith." This alone would have daunted most fifteen-year-olds, but I was looking for a faith, or rather a justification for my lack of one. *Ethics* was several metres over my head, but I persevered for at least ten pages till the language of pure philosophy defeated me. I returned to the racier prose of the Thomases.

Spinoza himself had no problems with philosophic abstraction. After Descartes, he read his way through the works of both the Jewish and Christian philosophers, and by his mid-twenties had formulated his own particular version of pantheism. It was a splendidly non-religious, rather than anti-religious, view that entirely fitted my own adolescent ideals and justified my own revolt. There was no need for any organised religion or worship. God was not above us, but within us. God is in everything and everything is in God. There is no point in ascribing to God any human form or emotions. God is therefore not the God of either the Old or New Testaments, not a capricious overseer who is swayed either by our prayers or those of our enemies.

After all the myriad dos and don'ts of Orthodox Judaism, all the horrendous hair-splitting of on-the-one-hand and on-the-other-hand, Spinoza's philosophy was a tonic. We are here, he says, in the same way that all God's creations, trees, fish, Shakespeare, or Socrates are here. Everything, from trees to Socrates, has a mind, but their minds have little in common, and all are contained in the mind of God. It is thus pointless for a miniscule human mind to question the mind or will of God — acceptance is all. Yet Spinoza's view was not merely mechanistic or determinist. An individual still has a purpose. Spinoza's analogies come from art. An individual is a note in a complicated and beautiful piece of music, a brush-stroke in a fine painting. Having just discovered classical music and Impressionist painting, I loved the idea of being the second "de" in the "de-de-de-der" of Beethoven's Fifth or the fifty-third red dot from the left in Seurat's *Sunday in the Park*. We are, said Spinoza, part of a grand design without knowing who the designer is, or what he is ultimately designing. Life is the more enjoyable for living with that mystery, rather than constantly fretting about it and speculating about what God wants of us.

With one philosophic bound I was free. According to Spinoza, we were born into this world to be happy. Happiness was defined as seeking pleasure and avoiding pain. Lest this seem too hedonistic, he added a perfectly logical caveat. If humanity is one body and one soul, it surely follows that no individual can hurt others without hurting himself. To injure your neighbour was to pluck out your own eye. Ethically Spinoza was firmly in the Judeo-Christian tradition, while theologically he was the ultimate monotheist, yet without the mumbo-jumbo of vengeful Gods and mystical Trinities.

It was an error of teenage judgement however to try to explain this to my father. He saw my conversion to pantheism as no more than a self-indulgent mixture of spiritual laziness, moral indiscipline, and the desire to eat *trayf* — shrimps, prawns, bacon, and other non-kosher items. I was merely using

Spinoza as a philosophic smokescreen to avoid going to synagogue and for playing football on the Sabbath. And my father, suddenly white-faced, was again threatening me with instant levitation as I pushed my arguments, or rather Spinoza's, a sentence too far.

If Spinoza appealed to a rebellious fifteen-year-old, his thought also struck a contemporary chord. Three centuries after he propounded his environmentally friendly God in a secular society, his ideals had again gained currency. Furthermore, his English near-contemporaries, the Metaphysical Poets, were suddenly popular again. At school we learned John Donne's pantheistic paean: "No man is an island, entire of himself; every man is a piece of the continent, a part of the main", which famously ends: "And therefore never send to know for whom the bell tolls; it tolls for thee." Hemingway's novel *For Whom the Bell Tolls* had been published in 1940, and was filmed in 1943. I saw it, the tears running down my cheeks at the end as a sobbing Ingrid Bergman was forced to ride away, leaving her love, Gary Cooper, to defend the gap single-handed against Franco's advancing Nationalists.

The post-War popularity of this "No man is an island" sentiment was a commendable attempt to learn from recent history. If we had all, so to speak, helped Gary Cooper in Spain, might World War II have been avoided? If we had stood up to Fascism over Abyssinia, or in the Rhineland? When Hitler invaded Czechoslovakia, Neville Chamberlain had argued that Britain should not become involved "in a quarrel in a faraway country between people of whom we know nothing". Yet the lesson we saw in subsequent events suggested that no country was too faraway, and there should be no people of whom we knew nothing.

In any event, the more I learned of Spinoza's life, the more I identified with him. In his early twenties he went to study the classics under Van den Ende, the great Dutch philologist. Van den Ende had a beautiful, blonde, and talented daughter,

Katerina, who taught Spinoza Latin, and inevitably he fell in love with her. Three centuries later, at age sixteen, I was having a not dissimilar experience. Admittedly my Katerina's father was not a Dutch philologist, nor did she teach me Latin, but mine was no less beautiful, blonde, talented – and not Jewish. I had met her at a schools' conference sponsored by the Council for Education in World Citizenship, one of several, then fashionable, internationalist organisations. I was already worried about how I would break the news to my parents that I intended to marry out of the faith, before I even discovered if my feelings were reciprocated. No doubt Spinoza suffered the same anticipatory torments. Worse still, he had found himself, small and impoverished, in competition with a fellow-pupil, tall, rich, and Gentile. His Katerina chose the Gentile. I was spared such unequal competition. Instead, after a few blissful moments – we held hands beside the Serpentine and once in the cinema – my Katerina emigrated to Australia with her parents. Any heartache I felt was compensated for by the fact that I would not now have to face my parents with the news of my intended intermarriage.

As it happened, I could equally identify with Spinoza on the social and theological front. By the 1650s, his views were attracting unfavourable attention from the Amsterdam Jewish community, and he was summoned before the elders of the synagogue and cross-examined. Their worst suspicions about his "dangerous doctrines" were confirmed. However, hoping his integrity was weaker than his intellect, they offered him a very generous annual income in return for his silence and outward adherence to the orthodox faith. Spinoza refused the offer and in 1656 was excommunicated by the Sephardic community. It was in this same year, and from these communities, that Jews were invited by Cromwell to settle in Britain, where there had been none since their expulsion by Edward I in 1290.

The language of Spinoza's excommunication edict bears fair comparison with its contemporary Papal equivalents. Spinoza was declared:

a moral leper, who, in accordance with the judgement of the angels and the sentence of the saints, is to be anathemized, execrated, cursed and cast out from the tribes of Israel. No one is to hold converse with him, do him any service, live under the same roof with him, or to read any document dictated by him or written by his hand.

No doubt having first threatened him with assisted flight, his father now disowned him. Moving into an attic on the outskirts of Amsterdam, Spinoza trained as a lens-grinder in order to make a living. He continued to study and publish his philosophical work, and as his intellectual fame grew, he was visited in his small flat in The Hague by the leading thinkers of the time. Poor and unmarried, he died there of tuberculosis at the age of forty-five.

To my mind, not a lot seemed to have changed in Orthodox Judaism from 17th-century Amsterdam to mid-20th-century north London. To avoid further alienation from my father I continued to accompany him to synagogue, where I would glaze over by the third hour. Ever since then I have been convinced that the length of orthodox services is far more responsible for driving young men away from Judaism than even the lure of Aryan women. While those around me swayed and prayed, when not exchanging gossip, I sat planning heretical pantheistic tracts. Though I couldn't imagine the worthy wardens of my local synagogue offering me any kind of regular income for my silence, I could be sure they would excommunicate me out-of-hand, and in far less flowing language.

The Thomases dealt with nineteen other philosophers in their *Lives of the Great Philosophers*, and I did not totally ignore them. In the chapter on Socrates, I was drawn to a fanciful idea put forward by Aristophanes in a Socratic debate on love, where he suggests that the two sexes were once united in one body: a body round like a ball, with four hands, four feet, and two faces. Using its eight limbs like the spokes of a wheel in a continual series of somersaults, it moved about with amazing rapidity. This race of men-women was incredibly strong and boundless in its ambition. According to Aristophanes, they were planning to scale the heavens and attack the gods, when Zeus had a stroke of divine genius. "Let us cut them in two," he said, "and then they will have only half their strength and we shall have twice as many sacrifices." And so Zeus split them apart into male and female, and from that day onward the two halves of the once-united body have been consumed with a longing to be reunited. This longing for the reunion of the sexes, Aristophanes concluded, is what we call love. It also happened to suit perfectly my own adolescent longings. Which is to say, thanks to Spinoza, Aristophanes, and Henry and Dana Lee Thomas, I was now a thorough-going romantic Pantheist.

11. Otherliness

With the War over, Ireland no longer played the same role in our lives. We no longer needed a safe haven, our family there was shrinking, and while we frequently went back for weddings and funerals, we now returned to our North London home, that tiny corner where the Irish and the Jewish diaspora intersected. Though I was never to live there again, my Irish background was to run through my life like a thin green line. Or, more accurately, like a long piece of green string, with me as the yo-yo on the end, being pulled back and forth by circumstance.

As my Grandma White's sight was failing rapidly, the time had come to sell the big house in Kenilworth Square. She came to live in London with my widowed Aunt Eileen. My mother was devoted to this elder sister, and I had come to resent her bitterly. Even when she became trapped in the traditional fate of the unmarried daughter looking after the ailing mother, I had no sympathy. It meant we now saw more of her and always with my almost-blind grandmother in tow.

On the White side there was only Uncle Michael left in Dublin with his wife, Miriam. They ran the shoe company, all that was now left of Grandfather White's business empire. They had a young family, two sons and a daughter who would at least keep the White name going in Dublin. The Prices were less fortunate. With Polly in her Surrey sanitorium, the two sisters, Minnie and Hilda, remained single and barely solvent on the South Circular Road. With all hope of rich suitors and remunerative employment long since abandoned, they continued with the *vekele* job that they had inherited from their father. They went out collecting their payments in a battered old Ford, until it finally wrapped itself round a tree somewhere in County Wicklow. The sisters were unhurt, and my father was obliged to buy them another, more recent, model.

The Girls in happier times – from left: Minnie, Hilda and Polly.

For my parents, the attraction of going to Dublin had clearly dwindled. It was still always referred to as home, but was associated now with bereavement and sadness, with good times long past. And it was in those early post-War years that I first became aware of my parents' complicated identity problems, of the Irish-Jewish circles in which they almost exclusively mixed, and the way they kept their past alive with a series of whimsical nicknames, tall stories, and esoteric jokes. There had been another influx of recently graduated Irish-Jewish doctors and dentists, and that highly esoteric grouping, the Irish-Jewish Graduates Association, had come into being. Most of them came through our living-room at one time or another, and for years I didn't think you could be a real doctor or dentist unless you had an Irish accent.

In those immediate post-War years there were two phenomena that deeply affected every Jewish family in the Diaspora. The first was the terrible revelations about the concentration camps. My parents preferred not to talk about these in front of us, deeming Ashley and me too young to be exposed to such horror. I read what I could find about them in newspapers and eavesdropped on conversations with morbid curiosity. Then one of my father's friends married a survivor. She came to meet us. It was summer and we had tea in the garden. She was an attractive woman and wore a short-sleeved dress. As she reached out to take her cup of tea, I saw for the first time numbers neatly tattooed on the inside of a forearm. I tried not to stare at them. It was the prelude to all the sickening horrors that subsequently came to light.

For my parents' generation of Jews, those who had escaped the Holocaust by geographic good fortune, there was an immediate lesson to be learned and passed on to the young. The German Jews were known to have had the highest assimilation rate of any European community. When Hitler came to power around a quarter of the Jewish population were intermarried. German Jews were known to their fellow-Jews in the Diaspora, rather contemptuously, as "more German than the Germans". Thus there was an almost sadistic glee when my parents and others said, "You see it didn't help them, did it?" The line of argument continued – when they came for you it didn't matter if you or your parents were intermarried. If you had one Jewish grandparent that was enough. It became the witches' warning to keep restless young Jews in the fold. The moral was – stay firmly within your faith, our paranoia is perfectly justified. Change your name from Goldberg, join their golf clubs, if they'll have you, sing Schubert and Bach, even marry a *goy*, but when the time comes you'll be in the cattle-trucks with all the unassimilated, non-golfing Goldbergs. It was a message history had made hard to refute.

In 1939, the world Jewish population had been 13 million. By 1945, the Nazis had virtually halved it. There are no figures for how many Jews subsequently lost their faith in God, let alone a Jewish one. Many no doubt did, but many more still kept their faith, or at least stayed identifiably Jewish. For most of these, Zionism became the answer and the British Government the problem.

In the Irish Jewish Museum, on the far wall as you enter, is a copy of a certificate to show that C.B. Price, my grandfather, bought one *dumin* of land (about a quarter of an acre) from the Jewish National Fund in 1927. This seems to be the extent of my family's early Zionism, except for the blue and white JNF tin collection-box somewhere in the house. A series of bearded men, sad, down-at-heel, and usually foreign, came from time to time to empty the box. My parents frantically stuffed coins into it before handing it over for emptying. This was a regular routine in most Jewish households of the period. As in many such homes, my parents supported the Zionist movement without sharing the dream of settling in the Promised Land. That was for others less fortunate or more devout than they.

I was not required to be a Zionist as well as an orthodox Jew, but I was encouraged to join the *Habbonim*, a sort of co-educational Zionist boy scouts. We wore imitation scout uniforms, short trousers and blue and white kerchiefs. We sang songs in Hebrew, danced the *hora* in bouncey circles, learned about the early history of Zionism and life on the kibbutz. Arabs were rarely mentioned, and little was said about the British Mandate. I found the experience embarrassingly hearty and alien. I was shy with the earnest girls, whose unflattering uniforms made them look particularly sexless. I didn't feel especially fetching either. I left *Habbonim*, using the time-honoured excuse of too much homework. I was confused enough trying to cope with the change from Ireland to England, from being an Irish Jew to being an English Jew. I might soon become something entirely different, but it wasn't going to be an all-singing, all-dancing Palestinian Jew under British rule.

Despite the Holocaust, anti-Semitism was still alive in Britain. Mosley's British Union of Fascists had resurrected itself and caused commotion in the East End. They revamped old libels – the Jews were running the black market, supporting their fellow-Jews in Palestine in the murder of British soldiers, and wanting to flood Britain with their homeless relatives from the Continent. Truth and compassion are not words in the anti-Semite's credo. As Conor Cruise O'Brien writes in *The Siege*: "People who disliked the Jews before the Holocaust generally didn't dislike them any the less because of it." It was a lesson it took Jews a long time to learn. At least in the East End, ex-servicemen and others in the Jewish Defense League fought back against Mosley's BUF, but the older, middle-class members of the community like my father stuck to the traditional Anglo-Jewish tactic of trying to keep a low profile, of not attracting attention.

This attitude was becoming increasingly untenable given the situation in Palestine. With thousands of pitiable camp survivors and other displaced European Jews clamouring to go to Palestine, it was not just Zionists who felt that the time had come for the promise implicit in the Balfour Declaration of 1917 to be kept. No time had been specified for the Jews to be granted "a national homeland", but if ever there was a time for the British Mandate to be surrendered it was now. The Zionists appealed, on compassionate grounds, for at least increased immigration to be allowed. President Truman endorsed the call for 100,000 Jewish refugees to be admitted immediately. The

British Government claimed this was impractical and rejected the appeal. At the subsequent Labour Party Conference in Bournemouth, Ernest Bevin, the Foreign Secretary, said the reason why America was pressing for so many Jews to be admitted was because "they did not want too many of them in New York". Bevin continued to enforce the strict immigration quotas. I shared my father's fury when we saw the harrowing pictures and stories in the newspapers of over-crowded and unseaworthy ships being forcibly turned back when in sight of Haifa.

The reaction to this hard-line British policy was an escalation in the activities of the Jewish terrorist groups, the Irgun and the Stern Gang. In July 1946, an explosion at military offices in the King David Hotel in Jerusalem killed ninety-one British soldiers and civil servants. Traditionally, Jews were victims, not murderers, and, in an editorial on the 26th July, *The Jewish Chronicle* wrote, "The Anglo-Jewish community has been profoundly shocked by this cold-blooded and abhorrent act." The Anglo-Jewish establishment may have quietly deplored the British Government's intransigence over the Mandate, but they had to go on living in Britain whatever was going to happen in Palestine. In the same issue, Dr Herzog, by then Chief Rabbi of Palestine, was more measured. He called it "a dastardly crime", but added "despair, engendered by a tragedy unparalleled in the annals of man, and by the failure till now of those in whose hands it is to bring balm and healing, has borne its bitter fruit".

As Jewish terrorism continued to increase, I noticed a growing divide between the Anglo-Jewish and the Irish-Jewish reactions to it. During the War my father had finally combined his Irish patriotism with British patriotism. When peace arrived, he had regarded the return of a Labour Government as an additional blessing. As a doctor in a working-class district in the 1930s, he saw the disastrous effects of unemployment and poverty at close quarters and became a keen supporter of a

National Health Service and its founding Minister of Health, Aneurin Bevan. But for his near-namesake "yer man Bevin" my father had a deep loathing. He was an anti-Semite and *Yidden-fant*, which translates as Jew-hater. He also considered him a class-traitor, a working-class trade unionist who had sold out to the toffs at the Foreign Office, who, as everybody knew, were a pack of snobbish, Arab-loving homosexuals. It was the only time I ever heard my father use that latter word. His recent British patriotism and that of his expatriate circle began to evaporate.

In their view, the British were reverting to type as an imperialist and colonialist power. They were doing in Palestine what my parents and their friends had seen them do in Ireland. The Palestine Police Force, almost entirely British, were just latter-day Black and Tans. As for the brave British Army who had defeated Hitler, it was shameful that they were now required to suppress nationalist Jews. Over my mother's tea and marble cake, mild-looking Irish-Jewish doctors said that in the end terrorism was the only thing the British understood, that without Michael Collins and the IRA there would never have been an independent Ireland. Of course, as doctors, they could not condone outright murder. They shook their heads with a not totally convincing show of disapproval.

Their analogy with Ireland was not so far-fetched. Both peoples, as Michael Davitt had pointed out fifty years before, had a history of oppression and religious persecution. To this history were now added further parallels, the broken promises of Home Rule and the false dawn of the Balfour Declaration, the horrors of the Great Famine and the more recent horrors of the Holocaust. In practical terms, however, the most important similarity was that they both had large and influential Diasporas in the United States, capable of exerting pressure on British governments. These parallels were not lost on the Irgun and their leader Menachem Begin, who had actually made a study of the tactics used by Michael Collins and the IRA against the British.

I felt closest to my father when he was at his most Irish. His accent and smile were always broadest whenever he railed against Lord Vogenschmeer and Lady Sweedlepipe, characters of his own invention. I never discovered the origin of their names, but they were protypical Establishment figures who epitomised the stiffness and snobbery he abominated in the British upper class. In such moods he became just another Dubliner who loved "a bit of gas" with a wonderful mixture of language, Yiddish, Gaelic, and English. In whatever language he used he never put a word wrong. *Le mot juste* came naturally to him. Only once did I see him almost at a loss for the right words. We had taken a boat-trip from Menton in France to Alassio in Italy. Returning late, we discovered the boat had sailed. Turning to an official-looking sailor, he tried his best in two languages he didn't speak: "Ou est il boatio?"

Apart from amusing Italian sailors, he was enormously kind and considerate to the unwell, the widowed, and the wallflowers of this life. This man was the father I wanted, not the one trying to observe the 613 laws of Judaic orthodoxy and imposing them on me. Only after he was dead did I see him in the light of those twin masks of classical drama, but at the time it was not easy having to live with both, loving one and not the other. Loving the whole of somebody has always been the hardest trick.

In November 1947, the United Nations voted for the partition of Palestine between Arabs and Jews, and the creation of a Jewish state. Six months later, Ben Gurion declared the independent State of Israel. After thirty years of thanklessly holding the ring between Jews and Arabs, the British threw in the towel, abandoning the new country to the mercy of five invading Arab armies, largely armed by Britain. There was now no question where the loyalty of Diaspora Jews lay. Some, mostly ex-servicemen from the Army and RAF, went out to fight with the Haganah, the Jewish underground army that had, with considerable ingenuity, been preparing for this war.

By an almost biblical miracle, the fierce fighting was over within six weeks. Those weeks altered the 2,000-year-old image of the Jew as eternal victim. Diaspora Jews could bask in reflected glory. My own feelings however were tinged with guilt. I was too young to fight, and I hadn't even stayed in the *Habbonim* and mastered the *hora*.

In 1948 no Jew could guess at the see-saw of emotions and loyalties about Israel that lay ahead. In the past, Diaspora Jews had only been concerned about the conduct of specific individuals or events. If someone called Cohen won the Nobel Prize, or only saved a dog from drowning, it was "good for the Jews". If someone called Levy burned his factory down for the insurance money and went to jail, it was "bad for the Jews". Now, instead of mere individuals to be proud or ashamed of, there was a whole nation in the Middle East to affect the ratings.

In 1948 I had heard of Arthur Koestler but had not read his books. Originally Hungarian, he was probably the most high-profile Jewish writer of his time. His reaction to the foundation of the state of Israel was to renounce his Judaism in an article in *The Manchester Guardian*. He took a coldly logical line. In his view the ultimate purpose of Judaism had been the return to the Holy Land. The whole point of the 613 laws had been to keep Jews separate from the societies around them, a guarantee of racial survival. With the existence of Israel, Diaspora Jews could now assimilate with a clear conscience. Emigrating to Israel was surely now the duty of any observant Jew. As Koestler himself didn't want to go there, and didn't believe in the Jewish religion, he felt it both logically and ethically correct to renounce his Jewishness. His public renunciation ended with a typically idiosyncratic point:

> No new-born babe has a say in the question to which denomination it should belong, and the usual practice in the world today is that parents who have no specific religious convictions leave the religious formation of their children to the hazards of the environment. I

believe it is essential for a child to start his spiritual development with a belief in God, regardless of whether this is a Jewish, Calvinist, or Wesleyan God, and to be left to make his decisions in matters religious when he reaches maturity. To put it bluntly, I regard it as an outright crime for parents who neither believe in Jewish doctrine nor live up to its commandments to impose the stigma of "otherliness" on a defenceless child who has not asked for it.

Inevitably both the orthodox and the more secular establishment sections of the Jewish community vilified Koestler. To those who regarded being a Jew as "belonging to a club from which you couldn't resign", Koestler's renunciation was ridiculous. One's Jewishness would be defined by the first anti-Semite one met. Prosperous Anglo-Jewry had no intention of learning Modern Hebrew, new skills, and going off to be pioneers in Israel. Nor did they want Arthur Koestler telling them that if they stayed abroad they should give up the lip service they paid their religion. The more enlightened admitted that Koestler had a point, in logic if nothing else.

Koestler's outburst merely fuelled my own confusions at the time. I knew about "the stigma of otherliness", that acute self-consciousness felt in so many situations in a gentile world. Even at home there were strange self-conscious paradoxes. On our front doorpost was nailed the obligatory *mezuzah*, the small hollow cylinder that contains a rolled piece of parchment on which is written the first two paragraphs of the *Shema* prayer – "Hear O Israel, the Lord is one …" This outward token made your house an irredeemably Jewish one. On the other hand, on Friday night, when it was time to light the Sabbath candles, my father insisted on my mother drawing the curtains, even in the summer when it was light outside. It seemed a combination of social embarrassment and atavistic fear – the candles would be seen from the street. If they couldn't be seen, then the passing Cossacks wouldn't know ours was a Jewish house. But what about the *mezuzah*? Well ours was small enough that the

Cossacks would have to gallop up to our front door to see it and include us in their Friday night pogrom. My father, it seemed, lived simultaneously in three time-zones, the good old days back in Dublin, the bad old days his parents endured back in Lithuania, and the confusing and uncertain here and now.

I totally agreed with Koestler about an infant's lack of choice and how the infant should be able later to decide what he wanted to be. I did not want to be an orthodox Jew, or an orthodox anything, but as my family were Jewish that was what I would remain. I did not want to go and live in Israel, but I wanted the country to survive and prosper. Today a majority of the world's Jewish population have that attitude and consider themselves secular Jews. And even half of Israeli Jews now consider themselves secular.

Yet being a secular Jew in Britain in the late 1940s was not so easy. For that, one needed to come from either an intellectual or Zionist-socialist background. Otherwise secular Jewish culture was minimal in the homes of the Jewish middle class. Just as the country as a whole was more church-going, so the Jewish community was more synagogue-going. There were special prayer books for holy days on our shelves and English translations of the Talmud, but little Jewish literature as such. Nearly everybody had *Yisroel*, a Jewish Omnibus, whose title suggested a segregated transport system. In fact it was an excellent volume of short stories from Jewish writers in eight countries. First published in 1933, it remained in print and sold steadily for twenty-five years, relying heavily on the barmitzvah market. Alongside *Yisroel*, there might be a couple of novels by Israel Zangwill, *The King of the Schnorrers* and *Children of the Ghetto*, and *Magnolia Street* by Louis Golding. Apart from these, no other English Jewish novelist or playwright had made their mark. In music, one learned that Mendelssohn was an assimilated Jew, and presumably various pianists with names like Rubenstein, Solomon, Horovitz, and Moseivitch were also, not to mention a string of violinists like

Menuhin, Heifetz, and Huberman. In politics there were some left-wing Labour MPs, and, of course, there had been Disraeli, which was a bit of a cheat as he had been baptised. Top honours, however, went to that wholly Jewish trinity of Marx, Freud, and Einstein, without whom the 20th century would not have been, etc., etc. The problem here was that our elders, who got such *nachus* (pride) from this trio, were hopelessly inept at illuminating for us any of the mysteries of Marxism, psychoanalysis, or relativity.

Led by *The Jewish Chronicle*, which called itself "the organ of British Jewry", my parents' generation played the ludicrous game of Jew-spotting, a not totally extinct pastime even now. It was another of those self-conscious paradoxes – while they wished to keep a low profile themselves, they took inordinate pride in drawing attention to famous "good" Jews. And so the most extraordinary names were conjured up. I always remember Mr Barnett, knowing my passion for the theatre, telling me that Sarah Bernhardt, apart from having one wooden leg, had two Jewish parents. These revelations of celebrity Jewishness were delivered in a way that conveyed a mixture of pride, envy, and slyness. The message, usually from parent to child, was "See. He became famous against all the odds. It can be done. So why can't you do it?" Also implied was how no Jew could ever keep his heredity secret from another Jew. An even further nuance was that it didn't matter who you became, you should always remember who you'd been.

Years later, I heard this very point epitomised in a showbiz story about Tony Curtis, né Bernie Schwartz, who was making a film in Rome. Late one night, in a highly excited state, he phoned an old school friend in the Bronx.

"Marty, Marty. Listen, there's something I got to tell you. Something fantastic happened. I just slept with Sophia Loren."

"So? For this you wake me? What's so fantastic? You're Tony Curtis. You're a star. Sophia Loren's your co-star. You slept with her. So what?"

"You don't understand, Marty. *I* slept with her. Me. *Me* – Bernie Schwartz from the Bronx. I just slept with Sophia Loren."

Apocryphal, I'm sure. Yet there could be another side to this story, if you remember that Sophia Loren was born Sophia Scicoloni and came from a poor family in Naples. While Tony, né Bernie, was calling his friend Marty, Sophia might have been calling her sister, Maria (by then Maria Mussolini, after marrying Il Duce's jazz-pianist son). Like friend Marty in New York, Maria is unimpressed. Sophia, like Bernie, protests:

"You don't understand, Maria. I slept with him. Me. Me, Sophia Scicoloni from Naples. I just slept with Tony Curtis."

She probably said it in Italian, but the moral is the same – you're never alone with an identity problem.

12. In One Bound

The end result of my divided education and loyalties was a series of lamentable school reports and exam results. By the time I took my O-levels, my parents were deeply pessimistic about my academic future. At the time the results were due out we all went to a wedding in Dublin. The bride was a second cousin much removed, so clearly any excuse would do for my parents to avoid being present for their son's academic disgrace. I was glad to hide away too. I should have been happy to be back in Dublin, but I wasn't. It was summer and few of my old friends were around, and those that were seemed scarcely to remember me. I kept thinking miserably of all I might have been, instead of a soccer-playing failure with an English accent. I went to the Joyce Tower, wandered around Sandycove, then walked to the end of Dun Laoghaire harbour and thought about chucking myself off.

Yet my mother must have had more faith in my academic ability than my father, for she had told Auntie Eileen to go into our house in London every morning and open any letter that looked like my exam results. Thus it was that my least favourite aunt proved the harbinger of my glad tidings – phoning my parents to tell them how well I had done in everything except physics and chemistry.

Twenty-four hours after thinking of chucking myself off the harbour wall at Dun Laoghaire, I found myself walking down it again with my mother and father. I had made them happy, and we had had a fine lunch out to celebrate. We reached the end of the long, wide walkway, one of the two curving sides to the impressive horseshoe that protects the harbour, with Dublin Bay in front and the Dublin Mountains behind. Choosing the most dramatic moment, the mailboat from Holyhead steamed slowly between the breakwaters, coming as though on cue. I remembered the times we had waited for it to come in, bringing my father over during the war. Now the boat was out there, and we were together here. We had survived torpedoes, bombs, and Doodlebugs, while the twenty-two miles of the English Channel had held the Holocaust at bay. It was one of those moments of adolescent clarity, when sights and sounds have a sudden intensity, and which sadly become rarer with age.

The mailboat sounded its mournful horn, and we turned and started to walk back. Taking my arm, my father said that now I had done so well, I should think seriously about medicine. But what, I asked, about my hopeless results in science? There were ways round that he said. For once I had the sense not to argue and spoil a good day.

Next day, our last in Dublin, my father played his trump card. He walked me round Trinity College. He explained that in his day it had been much cheaper to go to the College of Surgeons, as he and his brother Marks had done, but Trinity would have been much more fun, and they had always had a great rugby team. He remembered Bethel Solomons being captain when they won the Leinster Cup. He proposed that back in London I took something he called "a grind" in physics and chemistry. He was sure within a year I could do well enough to gain entrance. I would love my four years at Trinity and my hospital training afterwards, and once I had qualified I was guaranteed security for life.

We stood in the sunshine in the great courtyard of Trinity. It was like the top of the mountain, and I was being offered the treasure of the world – security. My father, as the devil, strove mightily to create his son, the doctor. I was sorely tempted, but reality asserted itself. I would have to "grind" at the same two incomprehensible sciences I had loathed at school, and then study medicine for seven years. I would have to cut up bodies and examine their offal. I would spend my days among the sick and ailing. It was a noble calling, but, alas, I hadn't been called. I said that I thought I'd rather study History or English.

What would I do with either of those, my father asked, his voice already getting edgy. My exam results had given me more confidence, so I said one day I might try and become a writer. He had done his homework well. What about Chekov, Somerset Maugham, Conan Doyle, and A J Cronin? he said. They'd all become doctors first. In fact, why didn't I think of becoming a ship's doctor and seeing the world. Then I would really have something to write about. It pained me to see my father so anxious that I should do something I knew I couldn't, and didn't want to, do. As we walked out of Trinity, between the statues of Goldsmith and Burke, two writers who hadn't been doctors, I lied and told him that I would think about it.

A potential "flying away from the table" confrontation was avoided shortly after by an unexpected intervention. I had had few dealings with Mr Haden, the headmaster of Mercers, but he turned out to have good antennae. He must have sensed some hidden problem which explained the discrepancy between my normal school work and the exam results. Probably even more suprising to him was that I had recently volunteered – never having volunteered for anything at school before – to enter the school scripture prize, which entailed studying the Book of Job and then writing several essays. Junior though I was, I came second to the head of school, who had the advantage of being a bishop's son. My secret weapon was all that Bible Study with Mr Barnett.

The story of Job also connected with a recent preoccupation. I had become morbidly interested in the growing horrors that emerged during and after the Nuremburg Trials. I had often in an adolescent way imagined myself in situations of triumph or disaster, shooting down

Messerschmidts, scoring winning tries, even, gruesomely, withstanding torture for a good cause. I had even tried to put myself in the situation of someone in a camp, but by no stretch of the imagination could I do it. I couldn't even get past the days and nights crammed together in the cattle-trucks en route. For its part, the Book of Job seemed to contain a private, individual holocaust, caused, and frankly admitted to, by God. Job had lost his herds, his land, his fortune, his wife, his children, and was afflicted, as a final short straw, with "sore boils from the sole of his foot even unto his crown."

And why? It was devilishly simple: "It befell on a day when the sons of God came to present themselves before the Lord, and Satan came also among them. And the Lord said unto Satan: 'Whence comest thou?' Then Satan answered the Lord, and said 'From going to and fro in the earth, and walking up and down in it.'" I loved the language, and the image fascinated me, as of late there seemed plenty of proof that Satan had been doing just that. A careless – or uncaring – God then boasted to Satan about one of his favourite creations, Job. "There is none like unto him in the earth, a whole-hearted and upright man, one that feareth God and shunneth evil." God should have known better than to tempt an inveterate gambler with good odds. Satan was quick to seize the opportunity – "Thou hast blessed the work of Job's hands, and his possessions are increased in the land. But put forth Thy hand against him now, and touch all that he hath, surely he will blaspheme Thee to Thy face." Of course God would have lost face if he hadn't now taken the bet. Hence the Book of Job.

Despite all afflictions, and even after endless, self-righteous lectures from his three splendidly named "comforters", Eliphaz the Temanite, Bildad the Shuite, and Zophar the Naamathite, Job never renounces his God. In just such an uncomplaining way did rabbis and other devout Jews go into the gas chambers reciting the *Shema* – "Hear, O Israel, the Lord our God, the Lord is one." I could not understand such faith. Despite my father's best efforts, I had never had it. Thirty years later, however, the story of Job provided an inspiring solution after I had wandered up a cul-de-sac writing a play. Those wondrous names, Eliphaz, Bildad, and Zophar, were waiting there to comfort me, as though learned only the day before. The play *Why Me?* went on to have a healthy and happy life in the West End and elsewhere.

When I came back from our trip to Dublin Mr Haden sent for me. My writing and its theological unrest had impressed him. Now a few quick questions exposed my domestic problems. He was no Job's comforter, but quickly came to the point. How would I feel about going into the Sixth Form – only at a boarding school? I heard myself saying I'd like to. A few days later he convinced my parents that it would be a good idea too. This was headmastering of the highest order.

Naturally my father would not agree to my abandoning religious observance so easily, but there was a possible solution. The same two Public Schools he had looked into earlier still had their Jewish boarding houses, serving kosher food. Once again Clifton was full, so once again it had to be the Perse in Cambridge, the very place to which I had once refused to return. I agreed to try it again, and, with Mr Haden's persuasion, they agreed to accept me. The prodigal pupil returned and, at sixteen rather than twelve, found boarding school a completely different and enjoyable experience. I was a senior boy, studying only the subjects I liked, and playing rugby and tennis instead of soccer and cricket. I began playing for school teams, and the housemaster looked discreetly the other way when I played on Saturdays. However, when this housemaster retired at the end of the year, the school decided not to replace him, but rather to shut the house. The school maintained they couldn't find another Jewish master to take over, but I suspect they may have decided that an exclusively denominational house wasn't such a good idea after all. Meanwhile Pollack's House at Clifton still survives as the only Jewish house at a British Public School.

In one bound I was free. Changing schools again was out of the question, so I became a day-boy. A bed-sit was found in the house of a Jewish lady who undertook to provide kosher food. A widowed German refugee, she was a highly intelligent woman who felt that I was old enough to lead my own life. This I now did for the first time. Saved by a shrewd headmaster, I was now inspired by a brilliant history master, John Tanfield. He had got a First in History at Cambridge, but more interested in acting, he had gone into Rep. After a distinct lack of success there, he transferred his acting career to the classroom, where his finest performances were playing numerous characters in the French Wars of Religion and Cromwell's Protectorate.

Free to organise my own extra-curricular activities, I took to wandering round the Cambridge colleges and quickly realised that I was living in an extraordinarily beautiful town. I also became aware of undergraduates. They appeared to be only a year or two older than me, and, blessedly, of both sexes. If anyone was having a better time than me in Cambridge, they were. My decision was easily and quickly made. I would read History at Cambridge, if they'd have me.

There were only two hurdles – passing the entrance exams and, if I did, convincing my parents to let me go there. The former proved somewhat easier than the latter. Gonville and Caius College gave me a place to read History after I had completed National Service. I went home to tackle my parents. The previous two years had been a period blessedly free of crises. Now a major one arrived. At one level, my parents were impressed, particularly as I'd been offered a place by two colleges. That is, until I explained that Gonville and Caius was only one college, rather like Fortnum and Mason's was only one shop. On the other hand, I could see that my academic success made them deeply uneasy. Clever children, they believed, went to a university to become doctors or lawyers. No one in the family had ever been to a university to study an arts subject. Nor, at that time, had any of their friends' children. They knew that they should feel proud, but instead they felt threatened.

To them, the very idea of Cambridge embodied the upper-class British ethos that my father found most inimical and intimidating, the world of his imaginary Lady Sweedlepipe and Lord Vogenshmeer. All his old Irish-Jewish prejudices reasserted themselves. Not only might I abandon whatever was left of my Jewish identity, but I might trade it in for a mess of Establishment potage. Whereas if I would take his advice and read medicine at Trinity College, Dublin, I might graduate into someone he could still recognise. Furthermore there would be family and friends there to keep an eye on me. He had heard and believed stories about Oxford and Cambridge being places where young people went "off the rails". Given my track record as a rebel, I was already a prime candidate for derailment. Then there was the question of the fees. On the basis of my A-level results I had been awarded a County scholarship, so that in principle my county, Middlesex, was obliged to pay my fees if I gained entry to a university. These awards, however, were means-tested, and any doctor's income would have been too high to qualify for a grant. I didn't want to be beholden to my father if he wasn't happy, so I visited the Middlesex Education Authority and explained my awkward position. They said it wasn't Middlesex's problem that my father didn't like History. What would happen, I asked, if he disowned me? I wouldn't be going to Cambridge, they replied. For years afterwards I only looked at cricket results to revel in yet another Middlesex defeat.

First and second-generation Jewish parents have traditionally been obsessed with the professions. Such jobs confer security and status in a society that is still not entirely to be trusted. My parents had no idea what one did with History afterwards – "Afterwards" being some mystical eternity in which you had to do something with History. I hadn't a much better idea than my parents about what I would do "afterwards". Maybe I could teach, and eventually try to write, but more immediately I just wanted to spend three years of my life at Cambridge reading History.

I was now in exactly the opposite situation to the one in Sandycove five years before, when I had locked myself in the bathroom to avoid going somewhere. Now I desperately wanted to go somewhere and had to think of a reverse strategy. Edwin Keppel Bennett suddenly sprang to mind. Known to everyone at Caius as Francis Bennett, he was the senior tutor who had interviewed me when I took the scholarship exam. About fifty, silver-haired, very dapper in black jacket, waistcoat, and striped trousers, he was the quintessence of an old-school Cambridge don. Even better for my purposes was his wonderfully kind, avuncular manner. If he could put me at my ease in such an interview, he might just do the same for my parents. I suggested that they go and see Mr Bennett and ask him what you did with History "afterwards". Amazingly, my father for once was not *shemadik*, and they agreed.

Shemadik is an extremely rare Yiddish word, not even listed in Leo Rosten's joyful *The Joys of Yiddish*. Best defined as what happens when excessive modesty combines with social embarrassment, it most frequently hit my father when he was forced to confront what he considered Establishment authority, either Gentile or Jewish. In such a situation he could cope only if he were fired by anger as a result of some injustice. His periodic attacks of *shemadik* infuriated my mother, whose reaction was always to say she would confront whatever it was on her own. Thus, to compensate for what she saw as my father's cowardice, she would go in all guns blazing. Invariably the result was disastrous.

My father knew they would get lost in Cambridge so he insisted that I go with them and drive. He had an *idée fixe* that East Anglia was perpetually shrouded in either fog or mist, and if he had to drive through either, he would get a migraine. We arrived, fog-free, in Cambridge, and I showed them the coffee shop where we should meet after their appointment. I then went with them as far as the first court of Caius College and pointed them towards Mr Bennett's rooms. As I watched them walk across the courtyard, our roles suddenly seemed reversed. I was the anxious parent, they the children, small and vulnerable, going into the unknown. I spent the next half-hour walking abstractedly on the Backs, oblivious of their beauty.

When they came into the coffee-shop, I knew everything was all right just from the look of them. Even before my father bestowed his highest accolade on Francis Bennett.

"What a gentleman!"

They had all had a nice chat. My mother was glowing with the experience of meeting Mr Bennett and how well they had all got on.

"Your father, of course, was too *shemadik* to ask him. So I had to," she added with pride.

"What?" I asked with dread.

"I asked him what you could do with History afterwards."

"What did he say?"

"He said," she imitated his surprised upper-class tone, "'What can he do with History afterwards? Mrs Price, your son will be an educated man.'"

Perhaps that was not the most insightful, mind-expanding answer to the question, but there clearly had been some alchemy about that moment, about the man who said it, the way he said it, and where it was said – as he had the most beautiful rooms in the college. Whatever it was, he managed to calm their fears by offering their son a future, some small share of the "afterwards". Maybe they realised that Mr Bennett, his college, and becoming "an educated man" were experiences they should not deprive me of. Or maybe it was just that they were from "dirty old Dublin", and their parents from *der heim*, and with his full head of silver hair in that seductive setting, Mr Bennett had held all the cards.

If you can walk on air, you must presumably be able to drive on it. Which is how I drove them home. There was no fog or mist, no migraine, no mention of *shemadik* again, yet my parents were strangely quiet. Maybe they had a premonition that everything they feared most was about to come to pass.

13. Khapped

There is another word that, suprisingly, is also not in Rosten's *Joys of Yiddish* – *khapper*. The sound "kh" is impossible to reproduce on the page in English, even phonetically. It is a version of "ch", but more guttural, more the sound made when you clear your throat, as in the German exclamation "ach". As usual in Yiddish, the word *khapper* has different shades of meaning according to context or inflection. At its mildest it means to snatch or take, as in "to *khap* the smoked salmon canapés first". More strongly, it means to steal, as in "khapping the silver". But there is an even stronger, more sinister meaning.

Czar Nicholas I, a military man who hated Jews, came to the Romanoff throne in 1825. He decided that the best way to integrate the Jews into Russian society was to draft them into the army. While national service normally began at eighteen and lasted twenty-five years, the Czar decreed that Jews should be drafted at the age of twelve, in order to do six years preliminary service. This "service" included forcible baptism, starvation alternating with the compulsory eating of pork, and sundry other sadisms. The recruiting officers sent out to enforce this policy were called *khappers*.

Their families regarded those boys who were taken away or "*khapped*" as permanently lost, and sat *shiva* for them. And their sons were rarely if ever seen again. They frequently committed suicide, died as cannon fodder in the Czarist wars, or if they miraculously survived, were so changed that they did not dare, or want to, come home. The *khappers* were meant to receive the cooperation of the Kahals, the local Jewish councils, who were given the task of choosing which boys should be conscripted. Later the Nazis copied this technique, leaving it to community leaders to select those who would initially be sent on the transports to the camps.

When news came of the *khappers'* imminent arrival, boys over twelve would be hidden, with some even inflicting mutilations on themselves to avoid conscription. In those years, shooting oneself in the foot was no accident. Whatever the precautions, some boys were always found, and if they weren't, the *khappers* frequently took violent reprisals. This practice went on for some thirty years until a more liberal Czar, Alexander II, eased the condition of the Jews generally, and reduced national service for everyone to six years. Yet it is not altogether suprising that Jewish families who fled Russia in the second half of the 19th century were paranoid for a couple of generations about members of their family being taken from them.

It is unlikely that my parents seriously saw the good dons of Gonville and Caius College as the contemporary equivalent of the *khappers*, but "taking away" has many forms. There is inevitably going to be a fear among all immigrants that their children will be seduced by the host culture. Immigrants live with divided hearts, longing to belong, but determined not to lose their past and their separate identity. It is a tortuous balancing act, but one greatly helped by religious faith. In this the Irish Catholic and Jewish Diasporas have always had a strong advantage.

My father took a rosy view of the cohesive, protective community he had come from. His Dublin was a warm and wonderful place. "Last year in Dublin" was more poignant for him than "next year in Jerusalem". His happiest day must have been the one when he qualified. He had achieved his chosen identity, Jew, Irishman, doctor. His coming to England however changed all that. He too was "khapped", though he was old enough, set enough in his ways and beliefs, to have found, in my mother's words "somewhere to hang his hat". And he was also delivered from the temptation to assimilate because the British Establishment of the day did not clasp young immigrant Irish-Jewish doctors to its bosom. He was happy to remain an outsider, but with his son it was different. By education, accent, even inclination, he was already virtually a member of the British establishment.

The latter-day *khappers* came for me by letter, a summons to a medical. If found fit, I would be required to serve eighteen months of National Service. My father had some worldly advice to offer, as once again the thin green line asserted itself. He suggested that I join the London Irish Rifles. I had the right credentials and it would "probably be good for a bit of gas". Given the lack of a London Irish-Jewish Rifles, it sounded like one of his better ideas. Especially, as just after leaving school, I had had a trial for the London Irish Rugby Club and played a couple of games for their 3rd XV.

Asked at the medical what my service preference was, I replied the Army and specified the London Irish Rifles. The officer-in-charge looked up the regiment in a reference book, only to drily inform me that it had been disbanded in 1919. From then on he treated me with suspicion. I was either a joker or a malingerer, if not actually a member of the IRA. If my career in the Army was blighted from the start, I knew who to blame.

Destined for the Education Corps, I was first sent to the Royal Greenjackets Brigade at Winchester for basic infantry training. In fact it often seemed more like training in basic language than anything else. For decades after, phrases and lines from incredibly filthy, yet euphonious, songs and verse wafted unprompted through my mind, their terrible, obscene poetry lingering long after I had forgotten how to dismantle a Bren-gun or hurl a grenade.

After a few weeks we were separated into sheep and goats,

and I was put in the latter group. I found myself almost entirely surrounded by the products of top public schools, a breed of which I had little previous knowledge. They were nearly all going on to Oxford or Cambridge after national service, and seemed for the most part confident, languid, and bored. No attempt was made to remember a name, rather they called each other after their schools. There was Eton, Wykeham from Winchester, Chouse from Charterhouse, Hurst from Hurst-pierpoint, a Stowe, and a Salop from Shrewsbury. If there was more than one from a school, they became Eton One and Eton Two. Coming from the Perse, a school they had clearly never heard of, I had the misfortune of becoming Percy.

They affected either camp or ultra-posh accents and coped with the barbarities of basic training as though it was some sort of Music Hall, or perhaps just an extension of boarding school. Stowe and Chouse Two worked up a simple double act which consisted of Stowe shouting out, "I say, any bugger got the time?" Chouse Two would reply, in his most languid posh, "Masturbation time." For ten weeks they never grew tired of this routine. Out of this whole mass of Vogenschmeers and Sweedlepipes, the only friend I made and kept was Hurst. Up at Cambridge, however, I would frequently be hailed on King's Parade with a friendly bray of "Hello, Percy. What's the time?"

What in *Tom Jones* are known as "vicissitudes", the Army calls "cock-ups". I experienced several, mostly bureaucratic, on their part. The first mistake the Army made was to select me for officer training in the Royal Artillery. It was the time of the Korean War, largely an artillery war, and presumably they needed more artillery subalterns. Artillery work is mainly based on the trigonometry required to line up one's guns on a target. Despite squeaking through at O level I was fairly hopeless at maths and told them so. They ignored this information, and I ended up on manoeuvres on the Welsh border in charge of four 25 lb guns and 16 gunners. Officer material that I was, I controlled my panic, did my trigonometry, announced the coordinates, and gave the order to fire. My – thank God – dummy shells winged their individual ways towards Cardiff, Swansea, Bath, and Birmingham. In Korean War terms, instead of killing the hordes of Red Chinese infantry facing us, I would have instead decimated the United Nations forces lined up beside and behind me. The commanding officer was most understanding, but thinking my officer material was better suited to the Education Corps for which I had been originally intended, he decided that I was to be transferred forthwith to their Officer Cadet School at Bodmin in Cornwall.

My transfer order came through from the War Office. I reported to Bodmin which is in the middle of a moor and probably looks pretty bleak even when it isn't covered in deep snow. There was another snag however. The Officer Cadet School had transferred to Beaconsfield, near London, a month before. The War Office didn't seem to know about that. I was told to stay there and await further orders. So I wandered around the skeleton camp, nobody quite knowing who or what I was. Because I wore leather gloves and still carried my officer cadet stick, various soldiers saluted me. It was not the time for long explanations. I saluted back.

After six weeks a sergeant who called me "Sir" marched me into the battalion office. My transfer order had arrived from the War Office. The commanding officer, the only person I ever met in the Duke of Cornwall's Light Infantry, asked me to sign the War Office form. As I leaned forward to sign it, the words "three years" struck my eye. I asked permission to read what I was signing, which clearly struck the CO as an unreasonable request. Nonetheless I read on to discover I was signing on for three years to take a short-term commission in the regular army. Appalled, I wanted to say that you'd have to be out of your mind to sign on for a day longer than necessary in the British Army. As he was clearly a regular officer I limited myself to saying that if I signed on I would lose my place at university. The CO said there were only short-term commissions in the

Education Corps. So I said I didn't want one. He asked me what the devil I did want? I said that I'd heard there was a sergeants' course. Could I go on that? He looked at me with loathing. Presumably officers in the Duke of Cornwall's Light Infantry weren't there to answer questions like that, or deal with creepy little displaced swots like me. What I had asked also required him to fill out more forms and send them to the War Office. I was about-turned and marched out of the office in double-quick time.

I wandered around Bodmin for a further six weeks, trying to stay alive in the freezing temperatures, my only duty to return the odd salute. Then I was quick-marched into the CO again. He scarcely looked up as I came in. "You will proceed to Beaconsfield." That was all he said. No "Godspeed" as he handed me the travel warrant. Then it was another about-turn, left-right, left-right, left-right and I was off to the sergeants' course at Beaconsfield. Both there and Bicester where I afterwards taught illiterates – there being a fourteen per cent illiteracy rate in the Army – were blessedly in easy reach of London and a girl I had recently met at a New Year party. Small and dark, she reminded me of Linda Darnell, a film actress I had written an adoring fan letter to at age eleven. Her name was Joanne, and to my intense relief, she turned out to be Jewish. She was in her last year at the French Lycée, and spoke good French. I managed to get up to London most weekends, and we went to French films at the Academy Cinema in Oxford Street, where we saw *Les Enfants du Paradis* three times.

My father's attitude to my military career was, as in most other things, paradoxical. He had two contrasting pictures of the British Army in his mind, the brutality of the Black and Tans, and the enviable smartness of British Army officers of that time as they strolled down Grafton Street. He was fascinated by their shiny Sam Browne belts, and I think he had secret hoped that I would wear one when I sat beside him in synagogue. Instead he had to make do with my sergeants' three stripes. While I was in the Army the whole question of my religious observance was temporarily forgotten. He didn't ask either what I did about the dietary laws. In fact I found myself eating everything, except pig in all its seductive forms. Bacon is always the last hurdle for the Jewish non-believer. I had been in the Army for six months before, being cruelly hungry, I allowed them put it on my plate to lie greasy and crinkly beside a fried egg. I sat and watched it for a while before finally succumbing, shutting my eyes and swallowing. Old superstitions die hard. I swear for a minute I was genuinely fearful that a divine thunderbolt would hit the mess hall, causing, miraculously, only one fatality.

My father was now forced to stop treating me as a naughty and rebellious schoolboy. I was a serving soldier protecting the country against the communist menace. Thanks to my efforts, if the Russians did come, they would at least be fighting British soldiers who could read and write. Nevertheless the paradoxes in my father's nature continued to manifest themselves. A fine example of this occurred when Ashley, now eleven, got into University College School, a liberal, non-sectarian day school in nearby Hampstead. Everyone was very pleased except my father, who seemed bothered by something that had come in the envelope with the good news. After lunch that day, he passed me a sheet of paper.

"Read that," he said, looking highly embarrassed.

It was a letter from the Headmaster, saying that all new boys coming to the school were expected to have had sex education. As many boys came to school across Hampstead Heath, they could be prey to exhibitionists and parents were asked particularly to explain this phenomenon to their children to avoid them being traumatised.

"That sounds very sensible," I said, passing the letter back. "You'd better tell him."

There was the sound of my father's throat being cleared several times.

"You – er – um – I don't know what he – er – um – er – knows. I'd rather you – er – um – told him."

"Me?"

Me? Me tell him? For God's sake, you're his father. What the hell's the matter with you? I mean, for God's sake, you're a doctor too. Why can't you tell him what men do with their peepees in bed and on Hampstead Heath?

I didn't say any of that, even though I wanted to. Instead of the contrasting masks of comedy and tragedy, here was another duality, the public face of the medical man and the private, *shemadik* face that couldn't cope with certain things. He pushed the letter back at me and I took it and showed it to Ashley later. It didn't seem to bother him. He didn't ask why it was me and not his father who showed it to him. I said something like "Do you know all about that sort of thing?"

He nodded.

I didn't want to make it sound too much like a session with my class of illiterates, but I think I did ask "Any questions then?" He was a little hazy about contraception. At eleven I didn't think he need worry too much – customs were different

Portrait of a laugh – myself and brother Ashley (right)

in those days – but I gave him a brief rundown. His only other question was, I suppose, inevitable and asked with some embarrassment. "Do – er – um – Mum and Dad really do it?"

"Yes," I said firmly, knowing that I found it as hard to believe as he did.

The eighteen months of National Service were increased to two years, but those of us who had places at university were allowed early discharge. I did twenty months in all, the last six months passing very slowly. Did I enjoy it at all? Not a lot. Did I benefit from it in any way? Well, I suppose I did. After all, it was in the Army that I had my first serious brush with the British class system, fried bacon, and true love. In the words of the great Ira Gershwin "Who could ask for anything more?"

14. Mein Kampf

The relief of demobilisation was so great that if Cambridge University had been a row of prefabs on the outskirts of Wigan it would have still seemed beautiful. Yet if aesthetically a delight, socially Cambridge was less of a joy. In the 1950s, there was an almost equal division between students from Public and Grammar Schools, from North and South, but, alas, not from both sexes. The ratio of men to women was ten to one, with nineteen colleges for men, and only two for women. Furthermore the last vestiges of the social attitudes I had found in basic training still clung on. For the first term or so, your school, regiment, and rank seemed a matter of importance to many fellow-undergraduates. After a few terms, however, past social glories faded, and a more egalitarian present asserted itself.

The first half of the 1950s was a strangely dead time politically. The reforms and optimism of the post-War Labour Government were long since over. The Welfare State was in place, but the problem now, as later, lay in paying for it. In 1951, the Conservatives were returned to power, and for my entire time at Cambridge, Churchill was prime minister. He seemed old, tired, and occasionally gaga. Attlee was leader of the Opposition. It was an odd, throwback period, in which nothing politically new or exciting emerged. Politics seemed to be marking time. For my part, I became a rather passive member of the Labour Club. With an Irish background and the recent experience of National Service, nothing could have induced me to support a party that contained any member of the British upper class, or in any way represented the Establishment. Most of my friends felt much the same way. We saw ourselves as a liberated, educated, class-less generation.

The non-Public Schools intake at university increased during the 1950s and 1960s, creating a social phenomenon that was little heeded at the time and captured in Philip Larkin's almost forgotten novel *Jill*. It was the social and cultural gulf now created between parents and children, one that frequently caused awkwardness and hurt on both sides. A further irony was that Public Schoolboys, who had an education and culture in common with their parents, suffered another gap, an emotional one created by all the years spent away at boarding school. Indeed it never ceases to amaze continental Europeans that in Britain the parents with the most money and the best homes send their children away, whereas in most European countries it is mainly children with major problems who are sent away to school.

I had, however, grown apart from my parents, culturally speaking, long before I went to university. There were still those shared, affectionate echoes of Ireland, but these had grown fainter the less I lived at home, and the challenges for me now all lay in England. At home, there was a truce in the wars of religion. During the vacation, I still made token visits to the synagogue, but my father never asked whether I attended in Cambridge. Nor did he inquire what I ate there. As Ashley was approaching his barmitzvah, my father's religious expectations now centred on him, but he was noticeably less rigid with Ashley, perhaps realising that one Bolshie in the family was enough.

In my first year at Cambridge I was having problems with another Jewish family – Joanne's. While still in the Army I had noticed, on their part, a distinct lack of enthusiasm for me. I was always amazingly polite and well-behaved with them, and couldn't believe Mr and Mrs Miller didn't like me. Perhaps they had heard of "the brutal and licentious soldiery" and were failing to make the distinction between a sergeant in the Education Corps and a rapist from the Royal Marines. I had hoped that when I went to Cambridge everything would be different, that Joanne would visit at weekends, and everything would be idyllic. She did manage to come a few times, but her parents made a terrible fuss about it. I was to discover moreover that their worries went beyond the possibility of a lost virginity.

That summer vacation I had a very uneasy cup of tea with the Millers. After some stilted conversation, I saw Mrs Miller give her husband a look that I recognised well. It was the same one my mother gave my father whenever she wanted him to speak up and he was suffering an attack of the *shemadik*. Clearing his throat, Mr Miller said, "What can you do with History afterwards?" Without Francis Bennett to help, I stumbled into a somewhat tentative impromptu "I think I'll – er – try to go into journalism." I could see that went down like bread rolls at Passover. The Millers were worldly enough to know that there was money in newspapers – that is, if you owned them – but they knew of no rich, successful, young Jewish journalists. All around them in North London young men were becoming doctors and lawyers, while even more young men were going into, even expanding, their family businesses and buying lovely homes for their beautiful brides. But their own besotted and perverse daughter, if she wasn't made pregnant meanwhile, after years of waiting was going to throw herself away on some impoverished hack.

Golders Green, Hendon, Hampstead Garden Suburb, those *stetls* of north London, were a far cry from those of the old Russian Pale of Settlement. There, study was considered a blessed task, a mitzvah. There it was considered a great honour if a student wanted to marry your daughter, and the parents usually agreed to finance their son-in-law's continued studies. But there the student would be studying the Talmud – and no one would dare ask him what he would do with that afterwards.

In the end the Millers forbade their daughter to see me, and when they discovered we were seeing each other clandestinely, they phoned my parents to arrange a meeting. My parents were not keen on the idea and turned to me for help. Couldn't I give Joanne up for a while so that all this fuss could be avoided? I don't think my father had strong feelings either way, and was just grateful that Joanne was Jewish. On the other hand, my mother had never liked the idea of my having a "steady" girlfriend. I should have lots of friends of the opposite sex, just like she had in the good old days in Dublin before there was sex. Then she became more personal. Five-foot, two-inches herself, she disliked being so short and, amazingly, disliked it in other women. Joanne was only half-an-inch taller, and thus qualified for my mother's disdain. And wasn't Mr Miller in confectionery or something? If I wasn't to marry one of the daughters of their decent Irish friends, she expected both myself and Ashley to marry a Rothschild, or at least compromise with a bride from the Sephardic aristocracy, a Sebag-Montefiore, or a Waley-Cohen.

I myself knew no good would come of this ludicrous meeting of Hendon Montagues and East Finchley Capulets. I could see my mother, at the first provocation, pull herself up to her full 5' 2" and let these miserable little London-Jewish upstarts know what it was to be Irish-Jewish and professional. And I would have loved to see my father pass through his *shemadik* phase and come out fighting, dander up, going from red hot to icy cold as he threatened to send Mr and Mrs Miller "flying away from the table".

I don't think much flying took place that evening. My parents came home looking wrung out, but they were not unsympathetic. They even wondered how a nice girl like Joanne could have such parents, but they advised me to go back to college and forget about her, at least for the time being. In the end it was Joanne who capitulated. She had to go on living at home with her parents, so I couldn't really blame her. I went back to Cambridge in a fury and took it out on squash balls, rugby balls, tennis balls, losing myself in improbable Jacobean revenge fantasies. I also started writing and acting, and about the only thing I didn't do was work. Eventually the crocuses came out on the Backs, and I began to feel better. The good thing about Cambridge was how quickly triumphs faded and disasters dimmed. Which was sad too – for it meant the three years would be over in no time.

Finally I started to work, and in the penultimate term I went to a party and danced with a beautiful girl. It was still possible in those faraway, romantic days to talk while you danced. She was intelligent, witty, and just small enough for my mother to dislike. There was another reason too why my mother would have disliked her. She wasn't Jewish. Her name was Judy and she was at Homerton College doing a teaching diploma. When I asked her out I detected a certain reluctance. She did turn up, but I discovered that the problem was she was already going out with someone else. At that point in the academic year that was par for the course. Anyway playing the waiting game suited my revision plans. I was trying to concentrate on the modern political philosophy paper and still had to tackle *Das Kapital* and *Mein Kampf*.

I couldn't cope with Marx's original writings, so I limited myself to secondary sources. Then I moved onto Fascism, and the crackpot prose of *Mein Kampf* which made pre-war British foreign policy impossible to understand. Surely it was the duty of British diplomats in Germany to read this book when Hitler came to power? And if they read it, how could they have had any doubts about what was in store for everyone? Surely reports should have winged back to the Foreign Office saying: "Dangerous loony in charge. Means what he says. Do not appease." Instead they tried to negotiate a sane deal with a madman, while selling friends down the river. I boggled at the lunatic lengths of Nazi racial theory. To fulfil their destiny of world supremacy, Germans must remain undefiled by sexual intercourse with other races, especially the Jews. The Nazis even suggested restricting tourism to protect their blonde Brunhildas.

While I read *Mein Kampf* Judy frequently strayed into my thoughts. "For hours the black-haired Jew-boy, satanic joy in his eyes, waits on street-corners for the unsuspecting Aryan girl, whom he defiles with his blood and thereby robs the nation." Wasn't that just what I was doing – waiting to defile? On the other hand, seen from the viewpoint of Jewish racial theory, weren't the Aryan girls, blonde and seductive, also waiting to rob our nation? Didn't my own, and friends', research show that it was easier to sleep with Aryan girls than Jewish ones with their puritanical upbringing. All such theories were, of course, repugnant, especially to a pure Pantheist trying to ignore all women and get a decent degree in History.

I managed a 2/1, decent enough, but now reality dawned. Finally it was afterwards and what did you do with History? The gulf between university and the life thereafter was enormous. The fashion of the time was to frown on transparent ambition, disdain the infection of commercialism, and prize a charming unworldliness. After all, at Lords, there was still the annual fixture between "Gentlemen" and "Players". In lieu of parental connections in the City, or, as in my case, anywhere else, we arts graduates made our way resignedly to the University Appointments Board. Declining teaching, industry, and commerce, I discovered that journalism, which seemed the best training for a would-be writer, was only possible if you were willing to serve your time in the provinces. I had never gone there before, and wasn't going to start now. An interview at Hulton Press, publishers of *Picture Post* and *Lilliput*, resulted in the offer of a job as a management trainee. The man at the Appointments Board said that if "one played one's cards right", one might eventually be able "to slide sideways" onto the editorial side.

Meanwhile my rival in love had done his cause terminal

harm. He had taken Judy to his college May Ball. For all its glamour and romance, a May Ball is an unrelenting marathon. It was the longest time that she had ever spent with this young man, and it was his undoing. Not that he did anything particularly wrong. He just bored her – for nine hours. I gathered that he also had a difficult and demanding mother. I had not at this point mentioned mine. Two days later, this demanding mum came to drive him home. Judy stayed on, and, in the true spirit of *Mein Kampf,* so did I.

"Going down" was a cataclysmic time for everyone. The end of our world was no longer nigh, it had nighed. I had no plans for the rest of the summer and no money. A couple of friends were going off to work for the summer at a funfair in Hunstanton, and they asked if I wanted to come. Serious work would start soon enough; a funfair might at least be fun. Judy didn't take up her teaching job till September, so I took a deep breath and asked her if she'd join me. She said "Yes", and we set up our first home in a tent in a field beside the Wash.

We were put in charge of a rifle-range with six rifles that fired small darts with coloured feathers for the chance to win some truly hideous prizes. The Education Corps had done nothing for my marksmanship, but Judy turned out to be a natural shot. Soon she was taking on American servicemen from a nearby base for side-bets. At the local cinema Doris Day was starring in *Calamity Jane,* and that's what the Americans inevitably called Judy. Between fusillades we talked. Her parents were separated, and her father, a convinced socialist and agnostic, had insisted on his two daughters being brought up without religion. I was grateful to him. It was refreshing to find someone with no religious baggage. I was only the third Jew Judy had ever known, and fortunately she had liked the other two.

After the long days and evenings we went to a friendly restaurant that let us in after-hours and served us their best steaks at a discount. Soon we were part of a small-town seaside

Mafia whose main purpose was to separate the trippers from their money. Such work was seasonal, and one had to make hay while the sun shone. Not that the sun did a lot of that at Hunstanton, but we didn't mind. We were happy there, and it was a terrible wrench to leave our tent, our rifle range, our American friends, and start our real lives elsewhere – and separately.

15. Time For Chapp

Auntie Eileen, who lived with and looked after my Grandma White, had by now, thoughtlessly, found herself another husband. My grandmother, virtually blind, was moved into a Home. After two weeks my parents' consciences got the better of them, and my grandmother came to live with us. Our household was completed by an Irish girl from Ballybunion, part-maid, part-carer, and Ashley, now studying for his O-levels. I couldn't cope with this return to the parental home and quickly moved out to share a flat with two friends in what was known as British West Kensington, the Caribbean immigration being then in full swing.

I found my first experience of earning a serious living utterly dispiriting. Nearly all graduate traineeships at the time were both ill-conceived and poorly paid, and most of my friends were having similar experiences. We moped around like the fallen angels from *Paradise Lost*. My main consolation was weekends when Judy came up to town, or I went to Oxford where she lived with her mother. On her starting teacher's salary she would have been able to afford little more than a closet in Cowley. And even if we had worked in the same town, living together would have been difficult. We didn't know any unmarried couples living together. Even Judy's mother's customary tolerance would have been strained by such an arrangement, and my parents would have collapsed in a screaming heap of outraged morality. In the summer we managed to go to Spain together. There, on an underpopulated beach, under a cloudless blue sky, the word "marriage" appeared briefly on our horizon and steamed across it, leaving a trail of small, dark clouds.

Judy understood the difficulties that "marrying out" would present her third Jew. Pantheism, the United Nations, World Citizenship, a planet full of miscegenated, coffee-coloured children with equal rights to life, liberty, and love – such was the post-War, liberal credo, and I subscribed to it totally. If I was half-a-man I would lead no girl, regardless of race, colour, or creed, up a garden-path unless it led at least to within sight of an altar. But I was only half-a-man, and the other half didn't want to hurt my parents – not that much. No one in the family had ever married out. None of their friends had, or their friends' children – yet. I had heard, but only in hushed tones, that some parents sat *shiva* if their children married out, just as their grandparents had when the Czar's *khappers* had taken their children. Marrying out was the final, mortal *khap*.

I began to hear voices, talmudically disputatious.

One voice said, "It's been a good experience. So stop now."

"Give up maybe your only chance of happiness?" said the other voice. "Don't be crazy."

"There are other fish in the sea."

"A fish in the hand is worth two in the sea."

"Not if it's not a Jewish fish."

"What's so great about Jewish fish?"

"They don't upset your parents. They guarantee the survival of our kind, for whom, like it or not, you have an existential responsibility. If everyone did what you want to do, there wouldn't be a Jewish fish left anywhere. Would you want that?"

"No, damn it. I suppose not."

A million such internal dialogues must have been going on then – before – since. Now one-third of the Jewish population of Britain has married out of the faith. Back then, I doubt if the figure was five per cent, but whatever it was, no one ever talked about it.

After a year's teaching in Oxford Judy decided she wanted to see more of the world and applied successfully to become an air stewardess. After three months training she was flying round Europe and North Africa. I was twenty-five and had never flown in an airplane. There was still a slight air of danger to flying, and I worried about her. My worry was not exclusively about her safety – there was also the threat of dashing flight captains and playboy passengers. Being a stewardess was still a glamorous profession, and after the Pyramids at dusk and the Acropolis by moonlight, a wet Sunday afternoon in British West Kensington might seem to offer less excitement.

Meanwhile my attempts to "slide sideways" onto the editorial side of Hulton Press were proving abortive. With my morale and bank balance equally low, I listened to the siren-song of a friend working enthusiastically in an advertising agency. He extolled the rewards of copywriting as a new and agreeable form of prostitution – the body and mind remained untouched, while only one's small facility with words was abused. I found an agency prepared to train me. After three months, my small facility was turned loose on a credulous public already in the first hot flush of consumerism. My pay doubled and I began to save with a particular end in view.

One day I took my mother to lunch in town. We rarely saw each other alone now, and she had dressed in her best. At her most vivacious, she acted like the mother I had always wanted to confide in. I was sufficiently disarmed to mention Judy to her. She had only briefly met her a couple of times and in general company, but she had acute maternal antennae.

"You're not still seeing her, are you?"

"On and off," I said. Ill-advisedly, I stumbled on. "I'm really quite fond of her." My mother reacted as though I had spilled my hot soup over her. Her eyes filled with tears.

"You wouldn't … you wouldn't …" She struggled to find a word she could bear to utter. She settled for "stupid". "You wouldn't do anything stupid, would you?"

I shook my head. The old hat now made an appearance. If I did anything "very stupid", she said, there would truly be nowhere to hang it. And beyond that, far beyond that, if I did anything "really stupid", it would certainly kill my father.

I nodded, looking as though I had taken her message to heart. Indeed I resolved there and then that I would never do anything "stupid" – not there in London, not there under their noses. If I was ever to do anything "really stupid", it would have to be a very long way away. A thought, or rather an address, crossed my mind – SB Chapp, West Orange, New Jersey.

Chapp, who called himself just that, as he loathed his SB which stood for Seymour Bentley, had married a grand-daughter of one of the two Price brothers who had sailed on to America when Charles Beresford disembarked seasick at Cork. I had first met him during the War when he had been stationed in England with the US Air Force. He was with an air-sea rescue unit in East Anglia, their job fishing out ditched air crew, alive or dead, from the North Sea. He rarely talked about it. He had been back since on vacations with his wife, Edith, née Price. Although Chapp was twelve years older than I, we got on well, and he was always insisting that I come visit them. However I had formed a more ambitious plan. I wrote and said I'd like to come and work in New York for a while. For that, a guaranteed job or sponsor was needed, and if he'd be my sponsor I'd guarantee to find a job. He replied by return saying he'd be delighted to be my sponsor. So Chapp became my American fairy godfather, in the days before "fairy" had any other connotation.

Judy had always been remarkably understanding of my parents' attitude to the survival of their species. She never took it personally, but she did feel that getting involved with a lapsed, but still conscience-stricken, Jew would probably prove one of life's major mistakes. Neither of us liked the idea that our possible future happiness would be based on someone else's pain. We had known each other for nearly two years and agreed that we maybe needed time apart to think it over. It would be painful, but over the duty-free wine and cigarettes that she brought back in fair quantity from her flights, we agreed a separation. I'd have been very hurt if she'd welcomed my departure, but she felt it made temporary sense. So did my parents. They felt that, with Chapp's help, I would find fame and fortune, not to mention a huge selection of eligible American Jewish girls, beautiful, rich, and, to please my mother, tall.

16. High Hair and After

1956 was a good year for heading West. In July, Britain and France were involved in the disastrous Suez campaign. The US shook a big stick, and Britain, France, and Israel withdrew. Colonel Nasser's Egypt emerged owning the Suez Canal. If the Suez campaign was farce, the Hungarian Uprising, shortly after, was tragedy. Central and Eastern Europe seemed irrevocably lost, the Cold War here to stay, and Tory Britain looked a thoroughly second-rate country posturing as something better. The British *Zeitgeist* was now discontent, and going west was in the air. What became known as the "Brain Drain" started here. It included, over the next decade, a number of young writers who wrote their American books – Malcolm Bradbury's *Stepping West*, Julian Mitchell's *As Far As You Can Go*, Kingsley Amis's *One Fat Englishman*, Dan Jacobson's *No Further West*, and my own *A World of Difference*. All the writers, with the exception of the poet Thom Gunn, returned. It was the scientists who went and stayed.

As I embarked on the boat at Southampton I felt that, even if I were two generations late, I was in fact only completing Charles Beresford Price's journey. As the boat hit the first Atlantic waves, I also wondered if I'd inherited my grandfather's weak stomach. Fortunately I took after his namesake, the Admiral. It was a five-day crossing and, by mid-Atlantic, I was experiencing total peace. No longer torn between religions, nationalities, or cultures, between my parents and a world of forbidden women, I could forget the past and ignore the future.

In mid-Atlantic there was nowhere to hang your hat, and it was bliss.

I had sailed on the Holland-America Line because their fares were cheaper. The one disadvantage, however, was that when you sailed past the Statue of Liberty and up the Hudson, instead of the excitement of turning right and docking in mid-town Manhattan, you turned left and docked in downtown Hoboken, NJ. Yet any sinking feeling I had was immediately lifted by the sight of Chapp waiting for me on the quayside.

After a warm welcome, however, he stared at my hair and said, "You've got high hair."

I had thick, wavy hair that had never caused comment in Britain. "Is that bad?" I asked him.

Chapp's approach was always very direct. "You can't walk round America with hair like that," he said.

It was the age of the crewcut in America, and all the natives were walking around looking like lavatory brushes. By nature a generous fellow, Chapp may have been worried that with high hair I would never get past a job interview, and thus become a burden to him for the rest of his life. We drove home via his barber in Newark. I pleaded with the barber as he cut to take it easy. He looked and sounded Jewish to me, but clearly he had Red-Indian blood. I came out pretty much scalped. Chapp was delighted and took me home to Edith.

"Doesn't he look great?" Chapp said. Edith agreed that I looked great. I felt like their pet hedgehog.

At college I had become a devotee of the Broadway and Hollywood musical, and now I had the wildly impractical idea of breaking into American musical theatre. I had two introductions that led to Manhattan penthouses but both came to nothing more than dry martinis and admiration for my cute British accent. I returned to my original intention to become a journalist. Mastering the art of creative CV-writing, I sent out dozens of job applications. I trekked in and out of New York for interviews, went to out-of-town newspapers in Long Island and

New Jersey and as far afield as *The Baltimore Sun* and *The Washington Post*.

My hosts were hospitality itself, but after commuting to endless job interviews from leafiest West Orange, I realised that I would have to tear myself away from the charity of the Chapps and base myself in New York. I had collected a few names and addresses before leaving London. A friend of a friend was a classics teacher in a New York private school. He had a room to rent in his Upper Westside apartment. I couldn't afford to take it and eat regularly, but he had a solution. I could give private lessons to his more backward pupils. I had forgotten most of the Latin I knew, so I telegraphed Judy to find me a copy of my schoolboy gospel, Kennedy's *Shorter Latin Primer*. A copy arrived by return. By staying a couple of pages ahead of my pupils, I managed to both pay the rent and eat.

One of my pupils, whose father was a vice-president of TWA, lived on the twenty-third floor of an apartment block on Sutton Place, one of the most desirable locations in Manhattan. One day, going up in the elevator, I became aware of the silent couple I was sharing it with. It was a miserable, grey day, yet they were both wearing large sunglasses. The man was very tall with a craggy face that looked rather like Abraham Lincoln. The woman, well wrapped up in a mink coat, looked as if she just might have been Marilyn Monroe. I stared for longer than I should have and realised that indeed she was, and the man therefore had to be her husband, Arthur Miller. As their whole demeanor spelled out how they didn't want to be recognised, I quickly looked away. They obviously lived above the 23rd floor, so we travelled all the way up together. I found it a terrible strain pretending to be unconscious of their presence. I made this uncomfortable, silent trip with them three times. The third time I tried a smile at Marilyn. It didn't come easily and must have looked like the rictus of a simpleton. She looked away.

I wrote frequently to Judy to report on the excitement of being in New York, even though I'd seen it all before – in the movies. To anyone of the cinema generation, much of America had a feeling of déjà vu. My introduction to the Hollywood musical had been *On the Town*. The story of three sailors on a twenty-four hour leave in New York, it was the first musical ever shot on location. I had seen it half-a-dozen times. I could have stepped out the choreography from the Battery up to the Museum of Natural History on Central Park West. I may have seen it all before at the movies, but there, on location, I couldn't afford to experience anything costing more than a couple of dollars. Despite my "cute" accent and Old World education, finding a proper job was turning into a marathon. For months telephone canvassing for home delivery of *The New York Times* was the nearest I came to journalism. And then one night I passed out at a party.

In those days New Yorkers ate dinner late and drank very dry martinis beforehand. That evening my empty stomach wasn't up to it. When my host woke me next morning, he said that before I'd been put to bed in the guest-room I had impressed the "back-of-the-book" editor of *Time Magazine*. For my part I vaguely remembered talking about the theatre to a genial, chubby man. Apparently I had told him that I wanted to be a drama critic. That was news to me. However I had realised by that stage in my job hunt that a vague Britishness got you nowhere in New York. You had to be very clear and specific about what you wanted to do. Dry martinis clearly brought out the specific in me. My host said the editor's name was Henry Anatole Grunwald. I had apparently agreed, before disappearing, to write him some sample reviews of new Broadway plays.

Unable to afford the price of a ticket, I discovered a recent Broadway practice called "previews". Tickets for these were half-price, as New Yorkers didn't like taking pot-luck before the reviews were out. Two reviews in the university newspaper were my entire experience of dramatic criticism before I launched myself on Broadway. I can still remember the three plays I barbed my shafts for – Graham Greene's *The Potting Shed*, slowish but fascinating, Feydeau's *Hotel Paradiso* with Bert Lahr, a brilliantly produced farce, and *Eugenia*, an adaptation of Henry James's novel *The Europeans*. It featured Tallulah Bankhead's last appearance on the stage, amazing and disastrous, and it lasted for only twelve performances. I sent my reviews to Henry Anatole Grunwald.

He saw me, complimented me on my style, but added that he was not about to fire the incumbent critic for an unknown twenty-six-year-old Englishman. He would, however, mention my name to various people in the Time-Life organisation. He kept his word, and over the next few months I was summoned to a series of interviews. I was beginning to feel it might be easier to become head of MGM and produce great musicals myself. Eventually the head of personnel at *Life* magazine offered me a job in the "cooler", a glorified mailroom that dealt with the photographs. It was, she said, the traditional starting point for aspirant reporters. I came out into Rockefeller Plaza, turned onto Fifth Avenue, and did a few Gene Kelly steps from *On the Town*.

No American movie, musical, or straight, prepares one for the climatic extremes of New York. The old Time-Life building in Rockefeller Centre was, by British standards, over-heated in winter and, amazingly, not air-conditioned in summer. As my main duty was carrying batches of photographs all over the building, my shirt was wet regardless of season. In this most sophisticated of cities, I was a damp, unglamorous messenger-boy working long unsocial hours. I waited impatiently for my elevation to most junior reporter in the finely graded hierarchy of *Life*. Some of my impatience was no doubt due to the fact that, back in London, Judy had beaten me to it as a journalist

I had received an angry letter from her about her employers, British European Airways. They were behaving, she wrote, like the Army. With the briefest notice they had posted her to fly out of Manchester, which meant living there. She complained.

Unbending, they said orders were orders, so she handed in her notice. Two weeks later, by a series of fortunate coincidences, she was offered a reporter's job on *The Evening Standard*. The postscript to this serendipity was tragic. Judy's replacement took over her schedule. The first flight was from Manchester to Zurich and back. On the return, coming in to land, the plane crashed, and everyone aboard was killed.

After five months at *Life* I was a deeply despondent Mercury, my winged shoes sweaty and worn down. Finally, and appropriately, on St Patrick's Day I was made a reporter. The thin green line in my life had appeared again, this time made visible in green paint down the centre of Fifth Avenue for the parade. On my first day as a *Life* reporter I took time off to watch the parade. My father had written to say I must watch because the guest of honour was to be that other hero, alongside Bethel Solomons, in my father's pantheon – Robert Briscoe. I had been reading about him in all the New York papers, which loved the idea of a Lord Mayor of Dublin being Jewish. I had also encountered disbelief whenever I mentioned that both my parents were Irish Jews. "I didn't know there were any" was the standard reply. Americans find it either confusing or comic when ethnic identities intermingle. The accepted wisdom is that the Irish come from a place that is green, good-natured, and full of drink and leprechauns. There are Jews there? They become Lord Mayors? In fact, Briscoe's son, Ben, served as a TD for thirty-seven years and was also to become Lord Mayor. His father had been a TD for thirty-eight years and they served consecutively for seventy-five years, a father-son record unlikely to be beaten.

The Americans took Mayor Briscoe to their bosoms. Mayor Hynes of Boston began his introduction of Briscoe to a vast audience with what sounded like a standard joke: "Once there was an Irishman and a Jew – and here he is!" as he gestured at Robert Briscoe. In New York on St Patrick's Day all the Third Avenue bars served emerald green cocktails, mainly gin lethally mixed with creme de menthe, but that year they were called "O'Cohens" and "Moishe Murphys" – and, most lethal of all, a "Bobby Briscoe".

As I made my way along the traditional route of the parade, it looked as though Central Park had spilled out in one night of phenomenal growth and taken over Fifth Avenue. Everybody and everything seemed to be entirely green. As the pipes of the marching bands drifted up the Avenue, I found a spot opposite the reviewing stand and waited for the first sight of my father's friend and hero.

Robert Briscoe's parents came from the same part of Lithuania as my grandparents. He had been an active member of the IRA during the Troubles. He had been fund-raising in the US and buying munitions in Germany. He was a personal friend of both Michael Collins and de Valera, enough to canonise him in my father's estimation. Subsequently Briscoe was also involved in the struggle for Israeli independence. On a bizarre visit to Ireland, Vladimir Jabotinsky, the militant Zionist, poet, and founder of the Irgun, had come for instruction on how to fight an underground war against the British. His heroes were also Collins and de Valera, and Robert Briscoe became his mentor. Briscoe subsequently helped raise money in America for the Irgun, much as he had done for the IRA. Prescient about the coming Holocaust, he had helped smuggle European Jews into Palestine under the Mandate.

When he appeared on the reviewing stand on Fifth Avenue, Robert Briscoe turned out to be a tall, dark, elegant man. I was close enough to see that he had a rather sardonic expression – that was till he smiled. When he did, his smile lit up Fifth Avenue. Beside him on the stand was the Mayor of New York, Robert Wagner, less suprisingly, also Jewish. But whereas Wagner looked a deeply worried Mayor, Briscoe looked as though he hadn't a care in the world. As the first green tide of the parade surged up the Avenue with a great skirl of pipe and drum bands, I suddenly had a huge lump in my throat.

Glancing round I saw other men and women looking very emotional. Some of the men looked old enough to have fought with Briscoe in "The Troubles". No doubt they were straight Irish-Americans, whose great-grandparents had arrived during the Great Famine. Maybe a few, like me, had Irish parents, but good Irish-Catholic parents. Suddenly I felt out-of-place, neither fish, flesh, nor good red herring. Was my mother right after all? Was this how you felt when you had nowhere "to hang your hat"?

I walked back through Central Park, trying to gather myself for my début as most junior reporter on *Life* magazine. It was only 17th March but suddenly it felt like spring – at least for me. I had come to America to make my own way, and I had. I had also come to think things over about marrying Judy, and I had. Despite New York and new friends, I still missed her enormously. Since the terrible plane crash at Manchester I couldn't help feeling her escape was a sort of message, a wake-up call – you don't know how long you've got, so make the most of it. I wasn't doing that however. Instead I was dutifully sparing my parents' feelings. They had been married happily for twenty-eight years, yet they and their beliefs were now denying me that experience. Was the survival of our tribe really so personally dependent on me? Living in "the land of the free" inevitably influenced me. Of all the freedoms – of religion, thought, the Press, false imprisonment, whatever – the freedom to marry who you want was surely one of the most important. You couldn't legislate for that though.

On that St Patrick's Day in Central Park I decided what I was going to do – unless, of course, Judy had changed her mind. I wrote to her and suggested that she fly out and see how she felt about it all – the place, the person. I knew it would be hard to ask her to give up her job on the *Evening Standard*, but I now knew for certain that I couldn't throw up my job, go back, and get married in England. Judy wrote back to say that she would try to get some leave of absence from the *Standard* and fly out in late June. Meanwhile I applied myself to the strange rituals of being a *Life* reporter, and the three months passed quickly.

Kennedy Airport was then called Idlewild and, on that longed-for day, I waited there in total panic. I had never been up in an airplane, and I marvelled how Judy, after that Manchester disaster, could get herself back into one. A combination of superstitious fear and Jewish guilt suddenly overwhelmed me. A vengeful Jehovah was going to strike me down. No, even more terrible, He was going to strike Judy down, because that would be a worse punishment for me. I would spend the rest of my life drenched in remorse. I found it hard to lift my eyes to the arrivals board to see if her plane had landed safely. It was delayed. I suddenly felt desperately ill. I was only twenty-seven and about to have a heart attack. Jehovah had changed his mind. He had decided to do us both in.

But then the plane landed. Judy came out into the arrival lounge. Her smile hadn't changed, nor had anything else. I was instantly restored to full health, and it was at least twenty minutes before she asked me, in the taxi, what the Americans had done to my hair.

After forty-eight hours Judy decided the place and the person were all right, and we set a date. There was only one thing left to do – to write and tell my parents. There was no way to break it gently. I tried to sound affectionate and reasonable. We had been apart for nearly a year, our feelings hadn't changed, and we were going to get married in New York. I posted the letter, and that was more or less that.

The night before our wedding, Chapp, who had been supportive throughout, called from New Jersey. He had received a cable from my mother. She said they had received my letter, and it had made my father ill. If I went through with the marriage, it would kill him. Chapp hadn't had an actor's training for nothing. He kept his voice totally neutral. He said the letter ended by asking him to do anything he could to stop me. There was a pause. "Is there anything I can do to stop you?" he said, voice still totally neutral.

"No," I said.

"I didn't think there was," he said. "We'll pick you up at three tomorrow."

As we were getting married at City Hall, we had been advised to book the last session of the day. The reason was apparent when we arrived a little early. We were the only white couple there and the only couple without a baby. Our witnesses were the Chapps and Judy's sister, who, quite by chance, had secured a temporary nursing job in New York. We stood before the registrar. It took us a moment to understand the strong Brooklyn accent when he told us to join our hands, but we did, and he married us.

And that was it. Judy and I lived and worked in New York, and we didn't hear from my parents for over three years.

Wedding, City Hall, New York, 1957. Cousin Chapp in mafia shades.

17. With a Capital "L"

In the late 1950s and early 1960s New York was an exciting and still tolerably safe city in which to live and work. Judy found a job on the sixty-sixth floor of the Empire State Building, fifteen blocks downtown from me, and I could see her window from mine on the thirtieth floor of the Time-Life Building. When it was cloudy her window disappeared, and if we were meeting for lunch she would phone to ask was it raining below on earth, and should she bring an umbrella? She was Assistant to the Iranian Minister of Information in the US. He appeared to have little information to dispense, and the only assistance that he wanted Judy was not willing to provide. We needed the pay-cheque, but after defending herself valiantly for a couple of months, she quit.

After a brief recovery period, Judy went to work at the Museum of the City of New York, where she edited a magazine for the city's schoolchildren. We had found a rent-controlled apartment on East 74th Street, and most mornings we walked over to Fifth Avenue. Judy got a bus uptown to the Museum, and I got a bus downtown. The Time-Life building had moved a block west onto Sixth Avenue, and I could no longer see her window from mine

Whenever I talked about life now, I had to specify whether it was with a capital "L" or a lower-case one. Both life and work seemed to require enormous energy, but New York had a strange capacity to revitalise – new energy for old. One only had to look around the city to realise that not all the poor, sick, and oppressed, whom the Statue of Liberty had welcomed to America, were made rich, healthy, and totally free, but a high proportion of them had certainly become very energetic. The British, whether at home or abroad, seemed lethargic by comparison. The downside of the city, however, was the number of loonies I encountered. I had never been anywhere that so many people spoke to themselves – usually mumbled racial profanities. Early in my stay, I had borrowed a couple of books from the New York Public Library. I was walking up Fifth Avenue with the books under my arm when a man in his fifties, by no means a tramp, looked at me and the books, then followed me for three blocks shouting "educated jackass".

Slowly and sometimes painfully, I learned the arcane skills of being a *Life* reporter. My prose was constantly fine-combed by the department editor for anglicisms. Why that mattered I could never understand as the much-edited prose of the reporters never reached the great American reading public. *Life* was a highly labour-intensive organisation. There were upwards of sixty reporters working for fifty or so assorted editors, not to mention the thirty or so staff photographers, most of whom had world-wide reputations. And all this was just in New York and didn't include staff in a vast network of domestic and international bureaus. I don't believe any press baron, before or after, has ever rivalled Henry Luce in the size or quality of the empire he created. *Time* and *Life* were the world's leading weekly magazines for news and photojournalism, and *Sports Illustrated* and *Fortune* were the same for sport and big business.

On *Life* the reporters saw all the action, going out on stories with photographers, and being responsible for all the interviews and reporting. We came back to the office, wrote everything up, at any length between ten and a hundred pages, all of which went into a research file. Photographs were developed, printed, cropped, and considered separately. When the managing editor finally decided to run a particular story, a layout was designed featuring the best pictures. Blocks of text were measured out, and these specifications were sent to the relevant editor to write – say fifty-six lines by thirty-seven characters, or vice versa. At this stage the editors then pulled out their reporters' research, staying in the office till all hours of the night or early morning, as they tried to fit the gallons of information into the pint-sized pots of text. It was not a task I envied them. A reporter was always on hand to provide any additional facts that might be needed at any hour, regardless of time zones. In a famous *Life* story, an LA bureau-man received his umpteenth query on a story about Cary Grant. It read "How old Cary Grant?" Finally exasperated, he cabled back "Old Cary Grant fine. How you?"

Despite the unsocial hours, I was happy with my lot. It was rather like doing post-graduate research at a high-powered American college. The other alumni were all university graduates in their mid-twenties to mid-thirties, and the male-female ratio was fairly equal, unlike *Time*, literally our sister magazine, where the reporters were all women and actually called "researchers". Always interested in film and theatre, I managed to work my way through domestic news, education, and special projects and finally into the jealously guarded Nirvana of the entertainment department. Both on and Off-Broadway were having exceptional seasons, and I had my first serious sight of Eugene O'Neill, Tennessee Williams, and Arthur Miller, while also discovering the first productions of Edward Albee and Neil Simon. *My Fair Lady* was still running, *West Side Story* had just opened, and other new and expensive musicals opened nearly every other week.

The Hollywood studios were enjoying a final flourish before independent production cut deeply into their monopoly of power. Complimentary tickets came in pairs, and we were thoroughly spoilt with the world's best entertainment. The only guilt I felt was about free lunches. It was awkward coming home to tell Judy of an interview with some star or other over a ludicrously over-priced lunch, especially as our own eating-out habits were more modest. Her work at the Museum might have been less glamorous, but at least what she wrote appeared in her magazine. And I'd have swapped any number of free lunches with Shirley MacLaine or John Huston to see my by-line in the magazine rather than just my name on the masthead.

One lunch, however, was memorable. About once a month Henry Luce held a luncheon for himself and senior *Life* editors to meet a distinguished guest who was currently in the news. The relevant department was responsible for the invitation and for sending their junior reporter to escort the guest to the penthouse dining room in the Time-Life building. As reward the reporter was allowed to eat lunch at the bottom of the table. The month I arrived in the Entertainment Department Henry Luce's guest was Marilyn Monroe and I went in the hired limousine to collect her at the Waldorf Astoria. Marilyn was then at the height of fame. She had just made *Some Like It Hot* and her much-publicised marriage to Arthur Miller was having an equally well-publicised break-up. There was a ten-minute wait before she came across the foyer. She was recognisably the woman I had travelled up in that lift with nearly four years before, in other words scarcely recognisable as Marilyn Monroe. She wore a long camelhair coat with its high collar turned up, a scarf round her hair, and large sunglasses. I was touched that she raised her glasses and smiled as she said "Hello". She had a lovely smile that disappeared as the glasses came down again. On the way out to the car a middle-aged woman recognised her and asked for her autograph. Marilyn, glasses still down, quickly signed her name on a bit of paper. The woman looked at me, paper still at the ready. I looked a bit young to be Arthur Miller, but if I was with Marilyn, clearly I must be somebody. I could see the indecision on her face.

"It's OK," I said, "I'm not anybody."

Marilyn and I got into the back of the car. As I sat next to her I thought of telling her that we had been almost this close together three times before, only travelling vertically rather than horizontally. I decided that would be gauche of me and require too much explanation.

Soon after having this experience I gave up telling people about it. My listeners invariably asked "What was she like?" The only answer I had was "Very nervous." It was not what my questioners wanted to hear but, sadly, people who are very nervous are not gorgeous, sexy, or alluring. I had heard that she became highly neurotic when making a film, and that was how she seemed going to lunch. She wanted to know what Henry Luce was like? Who else would be there? What would be required of her? I had only seen the world's then most powerful publisher once and he had struck me as a grim-faced old curmudgeon. I assured Marilyn he was charming and sympathetic, as were all the senior editors of *Life* magazine. They were probably more nervous about meeting her than she was about meeting them. "You're English, aren't you?" she said.

I admitted it.

"I worked with Laurence Olivier last year," she said. "He's wonderful."

My sharing a nationality with Olivier seemed briefly to comfort her. I told her that as a schoolboy in Ireland I'd seen him shooting the Agincourt scene in *Henry V* there.

"How wonderful," she said. She did have a rather little girl voice.

Going up in the lift at the Time-Life Building she reverted to very nervous again.

"I don't know why I agreed to have this crazy lunch," she said.

When we got out she asked where the "powder room" was. I directed her. "Don't go away. Please wait," she said. I waited. I looked at my watch. We were already twenty minutes late for lunch. I thought I ought to go and make some explanation to her host, my employer. I opened the door of the executive dining room and went in. Twelve pairs of eyes, including Henry Luce's, turned towards me. It is impossible to describe the expression on the faces of men who are expecting to see Marilyn Monroe in the flesh and instead see me.

"What's the matter?" Henry Luce said. "Did you lose her?" It was the only remark he ever addressed to me.

"No. She – is in the ladies. I think – er – she's – er – a little nervous."

Fortunately, one of the company was a woman, the Entertainment editor, Mary Leatherbee, a wondrously tough woman who had piloted transport planes during the war. "I'll deal with it," she said. She pushed me into my place at the end of the table and went out. After a tense five minutes she returned with our guest. Either Marilyn had taken something in the toilet or been hypnotised by Mary Leatherbee. She appeared much calmer and without her coat, scarf, and dark glasses looked almost like her publicity photos, though agreeably more human. She went and sat next to Henry Luce. Halfway through lunch I glanced up the table. Smiling and laughing, Marilyn had them all, even Henry Luce, in the palm of her hand. After lunch it was Mary Leatherbee who took her back to her hotel, but as Marilyn passed me at the bottom of the table, she said "Thanks for looking after me." I think I replied something as earth shattering as "You're welcome." Three years later she was dead.

Life was usually less dramatic in the rent-controlled apartment on East 74th Street where we lived – except occasionally Judy would tell me that Henry Fonda, who lived in the house opposite, had smiled at her. I had resolved that I would continue to write my parents once a month. After a while I knew I would not receive a reply, but I kept writing. It made me feel better. I kept off all provocative subjects, so what I wrote must have read like an impersonal newsletter. I didn't like to write Ashley as he was still living at home, but occasionally I dropped him a note. I would get a letter back, but I'm sure he didn't tell my parents that he had written. Apparently my name had not been mentioned since the day of our marriage.

The fact that the system didn't allow a reporter's writing ever to appear in *Life* provided the motivation to write for publication elsewhere. I sent some pieces to Malcolm Muggeridge, who was then editor of *Punch*. He published them and asked for more. It was welcome encouragement. I wrote some travel pieces for *The New York Times*. I was finally a published writer. Maybe now I should try to write a novel, only there was a problem. I was convinced that I had neither the creative originality nor the stamina ever to get past page 27. I had no idea why it was specifically that page – it was a totally arbitrary hurdle of my own making. One spring weekend, however, before the dreaded humidity arrived, I had an idea and sat down at the typewriter. Two months later I typed 28 at the top of a page. I had cleared my literary Becher's Brook and was still running. I wrote in the evenings and at weekends whenever possible. I was anxious not to make Judy so bored and lonely that she found someone else. New York was a positive jungle of predatory someone else's. I was amazed by the number of young divorced people we met and realized how sheltered our backgrounds had been.

It wasn't easy for me to be an ace-journalist, serious writer, and thoughtful husband simultaneously. A long vacation in a rented seashore cottage in Maine helped. There I found, for the first time, what a pleasure it was to have a large clear chunk of the day in which to write, while Judy caught up on American literature. In the evening we went out and, in childish bibs, ate incredibly cheap lobsters. One evening we brought two live ones home in a bucket. We had to drink a great deal to find the courage to plunge them into boiling water. By then we were convinced they were lovers. As I plunged them in the water we were sure they screamed. We vowed never again. Yet of all the places we saw in America, we always loved Maine the best.

Eventually the novel was finished. I found an agent, who covered herself by saying that instant success rots the soul. After several rejections the book was accepted by a British publisher, and shortly afterwards by an American one. My soul felt about right.

It was three years before I heard from my father. A strangely formal letter arrived announcing that my Grandma White, who still lived with them, had died. He suggested that I write a letter of condolence to my mother. I did, and she sent a rather formal letter back. I waited till the next letter to announce that I had a novel about to be published and that we were thinking of coming back to England for the publication.

In fact we were thinking of doing rather more than that. I had not been back in Britain for almost four years. Judy was getting ever more homesick and had a terrible longing for toasted teacakes. She did not have the excuse of pregnancy, but the idea of having a family had come up. We could not face the claustrophobic prospect of raising one in Manhattan, yet the alternative seemed worse. I had seen enough of the pitfalls of that solution around me at work. Couples moved out to the suburbs. Husbands commuted, spending long working days in the city, while wives stayed up in Westchester or out on Long Island, growing increasingly bored and exasperated.

Serious sociological studies, as well as more lurid novels, were full of the consequences of these situations. They dealt with commuting husbands who, after long tense days in the city, came home exhausted to their wives, longing merely to eat and sleep. Frustrated couples grew apart, and husbands were soon indulging in a custom that became known as "nooners". They slept with their, or someone else's, secretary over the lunch-hour, a time of day when the man might muster adequate energy and an available bed. This arrangement also had an interesting economic aspect. A secretary might have a pleasant apartment mid-town, but only if she shared it with several others to cover the rent. In the lunch-hour the apartment was empty, unless, of course, one of the other occupants had a similar plan. In that case a roster had to be drawn up. The plot had endless possibilities, comic and tragic. Billy Wilder brilliantly combined both in *The Apartment*. Meanwhile, out in the suburbs the poolman and gardener jokes had serious sociological significance.

The thought of sailing back to Europe had an increasing allure. There was also a professional reason. At *Life* promotion was closing in. The path to an editorship lay through one of the domestic bureaus. Detroit or Chicago had already been mentioned to me. I didn't like what I'd seen of the Mid-West, yet there could be a long wait for the more favoured Washington or Los Angeles bureaus. I enjoyed being a reporter, and promotion held few attractions beyond the larger salary. Becoming an office-bound editor, doing those complex text-box jigsaws of so-many lines by so-many characters late into the night, had no appeal. Soon I would be a published novelist, and I decided to be pushy. I asked for a posting to the London bureau and was told, in the nicest possible way, that English or not, novelist or not, there was no jumping the queue. I would have to work in a domestic bureau first. They knew that I wanted to go home for a while, and, being reasonable employers, they gave me six months leave of absence. Judy gave in her notice at the Museum.

Kennedy was now in the White House, *Camelot* was on Broadway, and politics and show business briefly intermingled. Bored with Eisenhower, and delighted to have seen the last, so they thought, of creepy Vice-President Nixon, liberal America was in highly optimistic mood. It seemed a time to stay rather than leave, but then homesickness reasserted itself. After all JFK would still be around when we returned.

As the *SS Flandre* steamed out into the Hudson from 49th Street pier, our feelings were incredibly mixed. We missed New York and our friends already. Yet, after four years, we were curious about life in England and anxious to try out married life there. And we had missed what we knew of Europe. Looking back from America, England had seemed only a small part of a continent. Americans have a whole continent to themselves, and when you've shared it with them for a while, isolationism can seem a perfectly understandable phenomenon. Cheap air-travel and international phone calls were still a thing of the future, and distance had isolated us too. There was no chance on our budget of a quick return flight home, given the price of transatlantic flights, and a phone call to Judy's mother was limited to a few minutes at Christmas or birthdays. But now we had earned the self-indulgence of sailing first class on the French Line. Celebrated for its cuisine, it was the same line Noel Coward always sailed on till he was banned. After landing in New York a few months before, reporters had asked him why he always travelled French Line. No doubt fuelled by their best champagne, he replied, "Because if the boat goes down there's none of that nonsense about women and children first."

In retrospect we were incredibly lucky to have spent those years, at that particular time, living in America. The country was in a sort of prelapsarian state, a brief historical interlude before the assassination of the two Kennedys and Martin Luther King, the long horror of Vietnam, and the humiliating scandal of Watergate. It was also a golden age of American culture. Their literature and drama packed a power and a punch that was subsequently imitated elsewhere. Their television was still innovative and watchable. On screen and stage they could sing and dance better than anybody else and nobody else had the joy of their jazz. New York was an invigorating place to be, full of a contagious energy and optimism that made anything seem possible. For years afterwards there was a noticeable difference between those people who had spent time in America and those who hadn't.

18. The Homecoming

Attempting a gentle re-entry into British life, we initially stayed with some old friends in West London. It was still a culture shock. Whatever we may have read about the social and cultural revolution taking place, things generally didn't seem that different from four years before. The "angry young men" may have seemed angry for Britain, but were still fairly tame in comparison to what we had seen and read of in America. The "Swinging Sixties" were slow off-the-mark, and our adrenaline gradually sank back to local levels.

On our second day in London, I phoned my parents. My mother answered the phone. The conversation is still with me:

"Hello, Mum. It's me – Stanley."

"Oh, you! Where are you?"

After not hearing it for four years, her accent seemed even more unmistakably Irish.

"In London. I told you we were coming over."

"Yes. We got your letter."

A pause – it was my turn.

"*We'd* like to see you."

"When?"

"Whenever it's convenient."

"Can you come for tea?"

"When?"

"Can you come today?"

"Yes."

"We'll see you then."

A few hours later I rang the doorbell and my mother opened the door. For a moment she looked at us awkwardly, and then we went into the hall. I kissed her, and Judy kissed her. My father then appeared. We kissed. A pause – and he kissed Judy. Whatever emotions were in the air were not otherwise on display. My mother had taken out her best china, and tea was ready. Over tea we talked about life in America and what we intended to do now. I asked about other members of the family, about my Aunts Hilda and Minnie. "Ah, The Girls – don't talk," he said, scratching the palm of his hand, a sure sign that nothing had changed on that front. They were polite and friendly to Judy. Our marriage, the long rift, what they had felt or we had felt, was never mentioned, not then, not ever. As we left they invited us back for Friday night supper. We drove away feeling indescribably odd.

Friday evenings seemed to be the time my parents expected us to visit them. My mother lit the candles and my father said the blessings over the wine and bread. We saw them at other times too, but the invitations for religious occasions were rather more formal. We were like a family slowly getting over some great catastrophe, except that we were the catastrophe. Nothing was ever said about Judy converting. Rather there seemed to be an unspoken understanding that she should observe them observing their religion. Three years worth of gefilte fish, chopped liver, and pastrami and salt beef on rye in New York's finest delicatessens had given Judy a taste for Jewish food. Now she could have it free at my parents' home, in exchange for listening to some Hebrew chanting on Sabbath and festivals. It seemed a reasonably civilised arrangement. She became familiar with Jewish customs, even acquired enough Irish-Litvak Yiddish to understand my father's jokes, but drew the line at learning Hebrew. After all, my mother didn't know any, except odd bits of prayers that she recited parrot-fashion. In her generation, learning Hebrew had been only for men.

A new relationship with my parents now gradually

developed. There was no underestimating the scar left by our marriage. Initially my mother treated Judy with slight suspicion but she gradually relaxed. My father was more open and friendly from the start, and his attitude to me had changed completely. He clearly no longer felt any religious responsibility. The worst thing a Jewish child can do to its parents had been done. I was beyond the Pale, so there was no good his worrying about it. In the end he had to accept my apostasy. Now his Greek mask of tragedy only appeared with the weekly arrival of the letter from The Girls in Dublin, or when worrying about Ashley, who was making up for my dereliction by studying to be a doctor. The trouble was Ashley was not doing it at a London hospital, but at Oxford, where our father suspected he drank too much, didn't work enough, and was probably subject to the terrible temptation to which his elder brother had finally succumbed. In only a third of these assumptions, the last, did my father turn out to be right. But for me, it was exit the stern Jewish patriarch, enter the warm, jovial Irishman, and in that role he had urgent need of me.

The annual dinner-dance of the Irish Jewish Graduates Association was imminent, and my father, by O'Buggins' turn, was this year's chairman. Though he loved telling stories, he had a terrible fear of speaking in public. I helped him organise his stories and craft the linking bits, but he was still scratching the palms of his hands a lot, a sure sign of a thornier problem lurking in the bushes. I guessed that the problem was Judy and I. Would they ask us to go with them to the dance? Our restored relationship had so far only been in the privacy of the immediate family. Could they face going public with it? Would it be our coming-out ball? In the end they asked and we accepted, though it likely would be as hard on Judy as on them. Neither Jewish nor Irish, she would probably be in a minority of one, but I had faith in the Irish ingredient of the mixture. They would make us feel at home. And so it turned out.

Having drunk several whiskies before and during dinner,

my father got to his feet with commendable steadiness. Kindred spirits, his audience knew what to expect and were with him from the start. They willed him through the time-honoured stories of the old days – of Jamie Clinch at his viva, unable to tell a right femur from a left; of the Irish XV "with fourteen Protestants and one bloody Jewman"; of the time his friend, "The General", fell into the vat of "black tar compound" in Hayes, Cunningham and Robinson's chemist in Ballsbridge. A few years older than my father, "The General" had joined the St John's Ambulance Brigade in 1917, in time to go to France and be in attendance at the Battle of Mons. On leave in Dublin, he was walking with my father and other friends by St Stephen's Green with the ribbon of the Mons Medal on his uniform. Two Boy Scouts, walking by, straightened up and saluted him. "Ah, the General!" my father and his friends immediately quipped. He was never again called anything else. Even his own children called him "The Gen". There were times in his speech when my father never made it to the punch-line, his infectious laughter having intervened. Afterwards the entire Irish-Jewish medical Mafia pummeled my arm and declared, "Ah now, wasn't your old man grand!"

We eventually stopped behaving like tourists and began to lead an ordinary married life in London. We saw Judy's parents, separately – them, not us. They were still not divorced though they had been separated for over twenty years. We rented a flat and bought a car. My first novel had come out, reviewed sparsely but well. Before I could develop another phobia about page 27, I began another one. We reckoned we could manage for almost a year on our American savings, plus an American publisher's advance. For its part, America now seemed like a strange interlude in our lives, sometimes very close, other times very distant. With the spring came American friends. We felt like an outpost of the Empire – theirs, the one that had replaced the British. Unlike the other natives here, we spoke their language and knew their culture, and felt our real home was probably Atlantis, that lost continent in mid-Atlantic – not a place to hang your hat.

The six months leave of absence ended without a decision. I wrote to *Life* saying I needed more time to finish a book. They offered another six months. Instead of New York we decided to go to Italy. Even if only for a few months I wanted to live the cliché of the English novelist on the Mediterranean. Through friends we heard of a villa on the coast north of Rome. It was available, and we booked it. The day afterwards I discovered my father had cancer. He had gone into hospital for a check-up, during which they found a tumour in the bladder. They operated and the consultant gave a hopeful, rather than optimistic, prognosis. My father was brave about it, my mother shattered.

My father's doctor, Dr Hirschman, was a family friend. When he heard that we were cancelling our trip to Italy, he proposed another solution. We should go, and when my father was fit to travel he should join us to recuperate. "Just my father?" I asked. Yes, he said, just my father. If my mother came too she would worry, fuss, and defeat the whole purpose. And she too would benefit from having someone else look after him.

I couldn't remember when one of my parents had ever gone away separately and was amazed when they agreed so readily. Dr Hirschman must have done a lot of talking. We went off and found Porto Santo Stefano, ninety kilometres north of Rome. We happened upon this small fishing village just before it became yet another over-developed Mediterranean resort. Already settled into a simple house outside the town with a wonderful view of the harbour, we went to meet my father at Rome Airport. He arrived looking frail, his case weighed down with the kosher chickens and salt beef my mother had insisted on packing. Judy felt she couldn't cook non-kosher meat alongside his, so we shared his supply, then all moved onto fish.

One Sunday we went out to lunch at a local fish restaurant. The people at the next table were eating platefuls of scarlet langoustine, those delectable Mediterranean crayfish. Thanks to my deprived kosher upbringing I have always had a terrible craving for shellfish, and I spent ages with the menu, tormenting myself about whether I could order some langoustine in front of my father. Would such flagrant flouting of his beliefs still upset him? Or was he now old and wise enough to accept my beliefs or lack of them? After all at home Judy had only served fish or his kosher meat. Wasn't it reasonable and honest to eat what we wanted when we were out? Judy and my father ordered sole. I ordered langoustine. My father made no comment then or later. I didn't enjoy my langoustine however and felt guilty for years afterwards. In fact I still do.

My father left after his two-week stay looking sun-tanned and fitter. The cancer was to remain, held at bay, sometimes painfully, for another ten years. It had become the fashionable psychological view that a child needs to say certain things to a parent before they die – a way of clearing the air, so to speak, for the living – I'm sure the good Dr Hirschman, a firmly practical South African, didn't have anything like that in mind for my father's stay with us. Certainly we didn't confide those feelings a psychiatrist might deem necessary for him to go more happily into the next world, or for me to stay more happily in this one. Such exchanges would not have been in the nature of our relationship, but those two weeks were the happiest time that we ever spent together. Maybe we reached the same goal by a different, quieter route.

Judy and I stayed on in Italy till our money ran out, and then we came back to London. Judy was pregnant, and the decision to remain in the bosom of the National Health Service had been taken for us. I wrote and thanked *Life* for their patience. Largely due to their training, I found I could earn a living from freelance journalism while writing novels.

That year, on the first Saturday in February, Ireland was playing England at Twickenham – the one day in the year when I felt most clearly my Irish identity. The kick-off that Saturday

Father and son, Italy, 1962. He always wanted me to be a doctor.

was at 2.30 p.m., but at six that morning Judy recognised the warning signs that she ought to head towards the hospital. It was snowing heavily as we drove, with incredible caution, across Hampstead Heath. Once there, the baby seemed to decide to delay its arrival till the snow stopped. I phoned my father to see if the match was still being played. He said it was, and why didn't I come and watch the match with him on television. I could just make it. I went back to check that Judy was all right and that there were enough nurses on duty. Twenty minutes later I was watching Ireland kick-off into a stiff breeze. It didn't matter that I couldn't really concentrate, as it wasn't a great game. Hands were cold, and at every dropped Irish pass my father flapped his own hand disgustedly at the screen and said "Ah, for God's sake!" At grosser errors of judgement he shouted "*Schlemiel!*" The final whistle blew on a scoreless draw, and I was up and into the car and racing back across Hampstead Heath.

At the hospital there had been a better result, even if I had missed it by twenty minutes. Our son weighed seven pounds exactly, and within a few minutes I saw that mother and baby were doing very well.

19. For a Crime Not Committed

My father died in October 1972. In the week afterwards, sitting *shiva*, I was constantly reminded of the effect of his speech at the Irish Jewish dance. Now, instead of coming up and saying "Ah sure wasn't he grand!", the same people were solemnly shaking my hand, wishing me "long life", and saying "Ah you must know, everybody loved your father."

Sons of famous fathers frequently find the comfort of the bottle preferable to attempting a pale imitation of paternal achievement. But what of the sons of men whose fame rests simply on being well-loved? Do we become desperate do-gooders, suffering fools gladly, goody-goody Samaritans for the rest of our lives? Or do we give up the unequal struggle and cross to the other side of the road, like the uncaring Levite, en route to drunken misanthropy? Ashley and I seem to have subsequently pursued a middle course, neither Samaritan, nor Levite, more sober than sodden.

Perhaps an understanding of my father's two masks helped in finding this balance. His friends and acquaintances had only seen the corners of his mouth turned upwards, only knew the *bonhomie* and the infectious laugh. They hadn't known how the demands of his God, together with those of his spinster sisters, had caused him such pinch-faced anxiety, such compulsive scratching of the hands. In any event, it takes time to realise how the relationship with one's parents doesn't stop developing just because they are dead. As a more tangible legacy, our father had left us four women to look

214

after – our mother and the Aunts Polly, Minnie, and Hilda.

Neither of us had seen Polly since that day, twenty-five years before, when Ashley and I had been packed off to the cinema, leaving her screaming hysterically on the landing. She died ten years after my father. Nor had we ever found out what had condemned her to the lobotomy and all those years in a psychiatric hospital. When I enquired once for her original admission record, I was told, with an apology, that papers that old had probably been destroyed.

My mother was to outlive my father by fourteen years. That first year on her own she was both sad and lost. Her role had been that of a doctor's wife, and for over forty years everything had revolved around my father's comings and goings to and from the surgery. My mother looked after all the domestic arrangements, and he did everything else. She would learn slowly how to lead her own life, but, naturally gregarious, she suffered terribly from loneliness. She took up oil painting, which simultaneously satisfied and frustrated her. A perfectionist, she loved doing it, but then she would worry that everyone else in the class was better than her, which in fact was only half-true. She suffered from both intermittent depression and the careless over-prescribing of tranquilisers and anti-depressants. On the whole, GPs don't have time to listen to the depressed ramblings of the elderly. For some it is easier to prescribe a hefty dose and hope it helps. In my mother's case it led to a serious accident.

She had always loved cars, preferably large, fast, and slightly flashy ones. She told us, proudly and frequently, how at seventeen, she had driven her father's Buick or Chevrolet around Dublin. But at seventy-five, dozy from sedation, she wrapped her little Austin round a lamppost in a dingy back street in Kilburn. No one had told her, or us, that she shouldn't have been driving on the medication she was taking. Although she recovered, driving was now out of the question. Like so many who have driven all their adult lives, not being able to do so took away her independence, and much of her morale went with it. She grieved for her car almost as much as for her husband.

This change was the start of a sad decline. In a constant search for something that would cure all her woes, she became pill-addicted. Possibly the doctors should have just given her placebos, but they didn't. In fairness she was not the easiest of patients. Occasionally I went with her to the surgery, where I could tell from the doctors' eyes that they didn't know what to do with her. And reading her eyes, I could tell she knew that they, as doctors, weren't a patch on her Jim.

We lived only five minutes away from her, but even with daily help, she took to besieging us by telephone. On one memorable morning she phoned while I was desperately trying to meet a deadline. Having taken, she thought, four paracetamol for a headache, she asked could she take two more? And, still constipated after umpteen Senokots, might she take some more? I tried, unsuccessfully, not to sound exasperated. I told her that writers did work sometimes – even though they did it at home. Anyway, wouldn't Ashley be better at answering questions about medication? "Your brother!" she sounded horrified, "I couldn't disturb him. He's a doctor."

When it became impossible for her to remain at home, we found an old-age home about fifteen minutes away. She had a pleasant room, and the place seemed as agreeable as those places can ever be. After six weeks there, however, she had a fall and went into hospital. She died four days later. We went to the hospital, Judy, myself, and the good woman who had looked after her in the final period at home. The bed was screened off at one end of the ward. The nurse asked if we would like to see her. I still felt guilty for not having gone into the bedroom to see my father's body fourteen years before, and had yet to see a dead body. I nodded at the nurse, who took me to the end of the ward, sliding a screen slightly back so I could go in. My mother, definitely dead, not sleeping, looked peaceful. They had folded her hands together on the sheet and placed a yellow tulip between them. I wouldn't forget that moment or the date – it was my birthday.

The Girls, now in their early eighties, still survived, still living in the small terraced house on the South Circular Road, bought by Charles Beresford Price in the 1920s, when it had been at the centre of "Little Jerusalem". Across the road was the stately Greenville Hall Synagogue, now a computer warehouse but with the Star of David still on its stained-glass windows. Up the road was Clanbrassil Street, which had boasted at least thirty Jewish shops. Now there was only one – Baile Erlich's kosher butcher. Nearly all the Jewish families had long since moved out to the agreeable suburbs of Terenure, Rathfarnham, and Foxrock. All around may have changed, but for Minnie and Hilda time had stood still. In winter the house was cold and still smelled of boiled fish. There was the same furniture and the same photographs on the mantelpiece, their parents, their brothers in their medical graduation robes, my parents' wedding, and myself and Ashley as children. Living as though still in a Russian ghetto, they had always feared attracting the attention of the authorities and so had never paid income tax or national insurance. Thus they never received any form of state pension. Probably the last surviving *vekele* in Ireland, they still went out in their car selling domestic goods from a suitcase and making weekly collections of the instalment payments.

We had paid for endless repairs to keep their car on the road, but it eventually coughed its last, so they hired a man to drive them round their "customers". Soon Ashley and I were getting requests for money to help pay John, their driver. On my next trip to Dublin I tried to find out how much they made from their business. They were as unhappy as IBM would be at having to divulge their business secrets. A quick look at their "books" however showed that any profit was being eaten up by the cost of John and his car. We were subsidising them, and they in turn were subsidising John to enjoy a couple of afternoons out in the fine air of the Dublin Mountains. I suggested that perhaps this was not the best way to run a business – that perhaps it was time for them to retire, and time for John to find other sponsors and companions for his rural rides. They were outraged. Give up their business! Let John down! What else would they do? It was all right for us over in London, but did we expect them to sit in the house all week doing nothing?

It was clear now that our money was not a contribution to running a business so much as to occupational therapy. Viewed in that light, it was a *mitzvah* (a blessing) for us to give. What the Aunts really lived off was the interest from a small investment my parents had made for them years before. That income, however, was diminishing rapidly in real terms, and they were beginning to live in real poverty. The house was now damp as well as cold, patches of mildew were appearing on the peeling wallpaper, and nearly everything needed repair. They were also both shopping and eating less. And so the battle began to persuade them into Ireland's only Jewish Old Age Home. The Home would have them, but they wouldn't have the Home, a sadly universal conflict continually repeated in so many Homes from home. Old age is one of nature's greater injustices. Instead of finally rewarding hard lives with strength, wisdom, and dignity, it generally dispenses exactly the opposite. As Anthony Powell wrote "Old age is like a punishment for a crime one hasn't committed."

As far as Minnie and Hilda were concerned, the fact that the Old Age Home was strictly kosher, in a pleasant Dublin district only half-a-mile away, and full of people they knew from the small community, didn't make any difference. Deeply conservative by nature, they wanted to continue to freeze and half-starve as they were. Letters flew back and forth, visits by Ashley and myself multiplied, and the help of community elders was enlisted. In a grand emotional finale, Hilda shouted, Minnie cried, and then they begrudgingly agreed.

When Ashley and I finally came to move The Girls, we had a strange and touching encounter on the South Circular Road. They were tearfully leaving the house as an old man, raggedly dressed with a silver crucifix round his neck, crossed the road towards them. I thought he was looking for money but Minnie and Hilda exchanged tearful goodbyes with him. Hilda introduced Seamus to us. For years he had been the caretaker at the Greenville Hall Synagogue across the road, now a computer warehouse. Despite this drastic changeover, Seamus had kept his job. While Minnie and Hilda climbed arthritically into the back of our hired car, he proceeded to tell us how he had spent sixty years of his life living and working on the South Circular Road.

As a boy, Seamus had been a *shabbos goy*, the non-Jew who comes in to light the fires and switch on the lights for the Orthodox on the Sabbath. In all, he had looked after the synagogue for thirty years. "Sure, I think I knew as much about your religion as the Rabbi," he said. "And now, at seventy-four, I'm in computers. Not bad, eh?"

We could see The Girls sitting in the back of the car sobbing, but Seamus had a final nugget: "And I'll tell you another thing. The Jews are meant to be so good at business? Sure they're not at all. A couple of years back, when there was hardly a *minyan*, didn't the Muslims want to buy the synagogue? And while yer men couldn't make up their minds, didn't yer men across the road sneak in and sell them their church." He pointed twenty metres up the road, to the late-Victorian Church of Ireland edifice I well remembered, only now with Arabic writing over its porch and a golden crescent on its spire.

Standing there, I felt a brief moment of pride. After millennia of being persecuted for, amongst other things, being altogether too shrewd at business, I was, even at one remove, now part of an inept Jewish business community.

"One lot go," Seamus sighed, "another come." We quickly agreed, not letting him elaborate. We said goodbye, got into the car, and drove The Girls away.

Of course The Girls never forgave us for what we had done. Whenever we visited them, they told us how unhappy they were. Fiercely independent and secretive all their lives, they clearly did not wish to share anything with their fellow elderlies. They took into the Home with them the roles they had played outside: big Hilda as the tough, angry protector of small, timid Minnie. By all accounts they gave the saintly Catholic staff a horrendous time.

Did they love or hate each other? Or combine both feelings in a love-hate relationship? Or was that too 20th-century for them? I had gained some insight into their relationship a few years before when I went in to thank their neighbour, Mrs Quirke, for all her help. It was a visit made memorable by a Malapropism on a very different subject. A red light burned in front of a picture of Jesus in her living room, and I couldn't resist asking what she thought of the then current scandal about Bishop Casey of Galway. Annie Murphy, an attractive woman now in her forties, had just gone public with the fact that she had been the bishop's mistress for years and now lived with their son in New York. Bishop Casey had been quickly shifted to missionary work in Latin America. The devout Mrs Quirke however was undaunted by it all, "Sure, I never did believe in the celebrity of the clergy," she said.

A great conversationalist, Mrs Quirke moved seamlessly from the worldly ex-Bishop of Galway to the equally sad, certainly more celibate, plight of Minnie and Hilda. "I feel so sorry for them," she said. "They never made anything of their lives." Despite living next to them for twenty-five years, she felt she had never really got to know them. "Hadn't I tried to help them," she said "but sure weren't they very proud?" Mrs Quirke was one of the few people whose words I always tried to remember and write down whenever I got home. She told of terrible rows next door, the two of them "going at each other loud enough to raise the divil". Mrs Quirke had wanted to go in and pacify them, "before one tore the other to shreds", but her dear, departed husband told her it wasn't a neighbour's business. "I think the poor dear was frightened that if I went in there, I might come back in pieces."

I let my pleasure with the "celebrity of the clergy" outweigh the other information Mrs Quirke had given me. Perhaps I didn't want to face up to what might be the truth about The Girls. Just as my father had never wanted to. All those weekly letters left leaning on the mantelpiece. Perhaps The Girls had been locked in their own version of Hell for all those years, and seeing no way out, had grown used to it. Maybe it was a portable Hell, and they had just moved it to the Home.

I didn't visit them often. As in most old-age homes, the majority of the occupants sat in the lounge with the chairs lined up round the walls. A visitor thus becomes the focus of a myriad of mixed stares, curious, envious, angry, or just blank. It is difficult enough to have any private conversation under these circumstances, but with Hilda there was the added complication of her now almost complete deafness. I would shout "How are you?" several times with increasing volume, and when I finally got through, I would be greeted with "We want you to get us out of here."

"Where to?" I would bellow back.

"Bournemouth," Hilda would shout. "We want to buy a flat in Bournemouth."

How they or we could afford this, or who would look after them there, was never discussed. Someone must have told them that Bournemouth had a very upmarket Jewish community and was thus an infinitely superior place to Dublin for two very old, very orthodox, fairly senile, Jewish spinsters. I didn't like to point out that they would feel as at home there as two rabbis in the Vatican. Rather I would try at this point to adjourn the discussion to their room. This was not always easy as Hilda had decided their room was not suitable for entertaining. In this she was right. It was almost impossible to find anywhere to sit, and if you did, it was usually on a half-eaten sandwich or banana.

They had filled the room with all their old bric-à-brac, and resisted fiercely when boarding parties arrived to clear up. The staff had retreated, their consciences clear, if not the room, with the knowledge than no one had ever died from an overdose of bric-à-brac.

The Girls shared an old Jewish superstition, maybe one common to all peasant societies, that if you make a will you will soon die. Not suprisingly, they hadn't and wouldn't. As with most old-age homes, the arrangement had been that all the proceeds from the sale of their house would be handed over. This already having been done, Minnie and Hilda became paranoid that the Home would next lay hands on the tiny income they received from my parents' investment on their behalf. The interest was paid directly into their bank, but they went to elaborate lengths, as though hiding a Rothschild-size fortune, to make sure no bank statement ever arrived for them at the Home.

To avoid all the bureaucratic problems of their dying intestate, I devised a cruel plan. There was only one authority they disliked and feared more than the Home and that was the State. I told them that if they didn't sign a will leaving their fortune first to each other and then to us, the State would not only tie it up interminably, but tax it extortionately. They were cowed by the threat. If they were to sign a will, however, they insisted on a witness who had no connection with the Home. The celebrated Mrs Quirke immediately sprang to mind. Ever helpful, she had managed to overcome her agoraphobia sufficiently to visit The Girls occasionally. It would seem perfectly natural if I turned up with her. Indeed the aunts' paranoia was beginning to make me think like a criminal.

The morning I arrived with the wills in my pocket and Mrs Quirke on my arm, the doctor was in visiting them. As we hung around their door, I prayed the doctor wouldn't give them too many intimations of mortality – which could bring back a dose of the old superstition. This train of thought was interrupted by an old lady grabbing my arm.

"I'm ready now," she said. "Come to my room."

"What for?" I asked.

"You know what for." She started to pull, and for a very small old lady she had a very strong and determined grip. I looked desperately to Mrs Quirke, who for once was at a loss for words.

"Tell me again what for?" I asked.

"Don't be silly." She sounded quite flirtatious. "For my feet."

"Your feet?"

"You said you'd do my feet when you'd finished with Mrs Heselberg."

"You've made a mistake."

"Oh no, I haven't," she said, pulling harder. "You promised you'd do my feet next."

"Tell her I'm not the chiropodist," I appealed to Mrs Quirke.

At that, the door of the aunts' room opened and the doctor came out. He looked at the old lady hanging on to me.

"Hello, Mrs Levy. How are you? I was just coming to see you."

"Not till I've had my feet done," she told him.

"All right," he nodded at me. "You do her feet, and I'll visit some of the others first."

"I'm not going to do her feet. I'm not the chiropodist," I shouted. Besides, she needed a manicurist as well, as her nails were digging possessively into my arm.

"Who are you then?" he asked.

"I'm Minnie and Hilda Price's nephew."

"Of course. Over from England."

"Yes."

"You're not a chiropodist, are you?" No doubt with his grand Irish sense of humour, he was finding it all more hilarious than I.

"No, I'm not a bloody chiropodist."

But the doctor was not a total Dublin eejit. Realising I was having a serious physical and psychological problem with Mrs Levy's limpet-like attentions, he took her free arm.

"He's Minnie and Hilda Price's nephew, Mrs Levy."

"I don't care," she shouted. "He's not doing their feet before he does mine."

She relaxed her grip for a second however, and I escaped. Grabbing Mrs Quirke, I shot into the sanctuary, if not the comfort, of The Girls' room.

The will was duly signed and witnessed. Four months later Minnie died. Superstition had nothing to do with it – she was eighty-seven and had been in poor health for years.

We were very concerned as to how Hilda would take Minnie's death. Whether it was love or hate, Minnie was supposedly Hilda's *raison d'être*. Everything Hilda did was for Minnie. If anything was not right in the Home it was always Minnie who suffered and Hilda who complained on her behalf, loud and long. Yet from the moment Minnie died, Hilda never mentioned her name again, never alluded to her in any way. All traces of her were removed from the room. It was as though poor old Minnie had never existed.

20. The Last Conversion

In late 1996 I was in conversation with a man I knew from Channel Four when the subject of my multiple origins came up.

"Irish Jews," he said, "I didn't know there were any."

"Good title though, isn't it?"

"What?" he said.

"I Didn't Know There Were Any."

"A title for what?"

"A programme about Irish Jews."

"*Ah!*" he said.

Thus the idea of my writing and presenting a television documentary on that endangered species was born. Of course, I was told, it would have to be a co-production with Radio Telefís Éireann, and, as is the way of these things, you could die of old age while the two companies worked out the finances. Eventually the uneasy Anglo-Irish marriage was arranged. However, RTÉ didn't like the title. "In Ireland we know there are Irish Jews," they said, "so it doesn't work as a title here."

"Fair enough," I said. In television I had learned not to argue with anybody till the money's come through.

Researching the programme I discovered some sad statistics. At its peak, in the 1940s and 1950s, the Jewish population of Ireland was around 5,000. Yet the last census in 1991 showed only 1,220 Jews in the Republic. Since then, several hundred, mostly young people, have emigrated – to London and Manchester, Boston and New York, Toronto and Tel Aviv. With the Celtic Tiger rampant they no longer had an economic reason for leaving. Instead their predominant motive seems to have been to join larger Jewish communities that might give them or their children a wider choice of husbands, wives, or partners. The anathema of marrying out, of causing parental anguish, is still strong, but there is also the anguish for these individuals and young families in having to choose between their Irishness and their Jewishness. And for the older generation, that choice means seeing their children and grandchildren grow up abroad while their own Irish community both ages and shrinks.

The problem of course lies in the exclusivity of orthodox communities, particularly when it comes to the highly emotive subject of marrying out. Shrinking communities are now a world-wide Jewish problem and an acrimonious debate goes on between the proponents of exclusivity and inclusivity. In the United States, where Liberal-Progressive and Conservative (in name only) synagogues are in the majority, a more inclusive approach has been adopted on all fronts. With more than a forty per cent intermarriage rate, this policy seems the only possible one for halting dwindling numbers. This approach is slowly and painfully being considered elsewhere, but in Europe, it remains a major thorn in the side of relations between the orthodox and the progressive synagogues. There is also an additional poignancy in Ireland, where if you talk of the problems of intermarriage, people assume you mean Catholics marrying Protestants. No one has yet done a comparative study of which causes the most upset in families – a Catholic marrying a Protestant, especially in the North, or a Jew marrying a non-Jew, anywhere. Perhaps a doctoral thesis one day – except on what Richter scale does one measure familial earthquakes?

For Jews, however, emigration for marital rather than the traditional economic reasons does not always provide a happy ending. There are Irish families who have sold up homes and businesses to live in Manchester's large Jewish community. Their children have gone off to British universities, fallen in love inappropriately, and consequently married out. *Amor*, as they say, *vincit omnia*. It would have certainly saved expense and upheaval had they stayed at home and gone to Trinity or UCD. By the law of averages, some of them at least would have married in, rather than out, and gone on to produce other Irish Jews for other Irish-Jewish children to marry. But I – as my mother used to say – am a fine one to talk.

A couple of years ago Judy and I were invited to a proper Friday night supper, lighted candles, chopped herring, gefilte fish, both fried and boiled, by an Irish Jewish family. Their eldest daughter had married an Irish Catholic and her father, our host, had not spoken to her for four years. They were now reconciled, but he obviously felt a need that evening to talk about it. Interestingly, it was Judy he chose to confide in. I saw him put his hand on her arm. Later she told me that there were tears in his eyes when he said, "Those were the four most wasted years of my life."

Ironically, the 5,000 Jews of my early days in Dublin have been replaced by three times that number of Muslims. Mosques have opened or are being built while synagogues close. At the time of making the film, the mock Byzantine splendours of Adelaide Road Synagogue were being enjoyed on the Sabbath by only 30 or so congregants, although its membership stood at around 400. Running costs were high and there was much talk of selling the building, which occupies a prime site in Central Dublin with a rumoured value of around £3 million. Inevitably, as in any religious community, there were huge and bitter divisions about what to do. One faction wanted to take the money and run – to Terenure synagogue where the two congregations might combine to form a small but very rich community. The older, nostalgic, and more traditionalist members seemed prepared to fight to the death for their hundred-year-old synagogue, where four generations of their families had worshipped. Only the Progressive synagogue in Rathgar, with its women ministers and men and women sitting together, seemed to be just about holding its own with a steady membership of 90 families, around 250 people all told. They'd even had some recent converts, and not exclusively of non-Jews wishing to marry in.

Other Dublin institutions were forced to adapt to changing times and the shrinking community. The Zion School in Bloomfield Avenue had been Dublin's first Jewish school, built partially with a government grant and opened in 1934. In the early 60s Maeve Binchy taught French there and was so popular that when she left the school's farewell present to her was a trip to Israel. "That was the start of my writing career," she remembers gratefully. The school closed in 1980. More ambitiously in 1952 Stratford College had been founded to combine a secular with a religious education, and flourished. A Rabbi taught Hebrew and religious education, and mostly non-Jewish teachers taught the secular subjects. By 1982, however, student numbers had dropped to a non-viable level, and the school went ecumenical. Now only a third of its 300 pupils are Jewish. Edmondstown Golf Club, founded in 1944 as a reaction to discrimination at other clubs, went through an identical process. In 1984 it introduced a new open membership policy and by 1997 the numbers of Jews and Gentiles playing there were roughly even.

Outside Dublin there was only one other Jewish community – just. In Cork, where Charles Beresford Price landed, the community was on the verge of extinction. There were virtually no practicing Jews left in the town, but its small, simple synagogue, on the edge of what used to be called "Jewtown", had been kept alive by the energies of two men, Gerald Goldberg and Freddy Rosehill. The former, the eighty-six-year-old ex-Mayor, had just handed over his headship of "the community" to Freddy Rosehill. Both men had the Corkman's typical view of Dubliners, especially, in their case,

Dublin Jews, whom they considered to have been always high-handed and neglectful of their community. It was thus particularly galling for them in those years when they only managed to open the synagogue for the annual Holydays by paying for eight young Dubliners to come to Cork and make up a *minyan*. It was an extra atonement for the Day of the Atonement.

And, fifty miles from Cork, Stuart Clein was the last Jew in Limerick.

I discovered that the national community was completed by an unusual group of foreign and nomadic Jews, a small band of Israeli ritual slaughterers (*shochotim*), who slit the throats and drain the blood from best-quality animals for the large Irish export trade in kosher meat to the rest of Europe and Israel. Together they move between the abattoirs of Kildare, Wexford, and Limerick. Highly orthodox, they never travel in a group of less than ten so that they can hold morning and evening services at either end of the day's slaughtering. Is it possible that within another generation or two the indigenous Jewish population will have died out, and the only Jews left in Ireland will be a marauding band of Israeli slaughterers? Will the legacy of my Litvak grandparents, and a thousand like them, merely be the provision of meat to kosher butchers in the European Union? It would be truly ironic if an Irish-Jewish community that had identified so much with its host country, and survived its bad times, should disappear just as the good times roll.

Apart from contrasting the Ireland of my youth with that of today, making the documentary was also an opportunity to tell of my quest for the origins of Charles Beresford Price. I had dramatised part of the film, so we needed two actors to play my parents and a twelve-year-old who was both Jewish and good at rugby, and thereby able to look at home both in a synagogue and on the rugby field. We found Alex Feldman, who played scrum-half for High School Under-13s. And so I had the unnerving experience of watching these approximations of myself and my parents doing that Saturday walk, from the comforts of Kenilworth Square to the boiled plaice of Dolphin's Barn.

Then it was off to Lansdowne Road, which the Irish Rugby Union had kindly lent us for a couple of hours one morning. The idea was that I would be filmed in the stand, watching my young alter ego diving over the line for that great try and then kicking the winning conversion. Fifty years before on St Stephen's Green, Bethel Solomons had patted me on the shoulder, saying he would look out for me at Lansdowne Road. Well, here I finally was, not in the green shirt with the shamrock, running in the winning try, but in a blue anorak, alone in the stand. Below me a twelve-year-old schoolboy scored that try, then kicked the conversion unopposed on an empty field for the benefit of the camera. Just so I could boast to my brother, I went down and walked on the sacred turf. Alex threw the ball to me. Fortunately I managed to catch it. Suddenly I was gripped by the daemon of rugby, or maybe it was the ghost of Jamie Clinch, that great centre who couldn't tell his right femur from his left. Out on the twenty-two, not quite in front of the posts, I made a dent with my heel and stood the ball up at the right angle. The score was Ireland 10, England 10. It was the last kick of the match. I took three steps back. For a moment I was Ronan O'Gara. Relaxing my body, I glanced up at the posts and then, eyes down, in my ordinary walking shoes, I ran up and elegantly stroked the ball towards the posts. It fell well short and to the right. As well as Alex, a groundsman had been watching. All I had proved was that you can make a fool of yourself at any age. I wouldn't be telling Ashley about that.

The groundsman recovered the ball. "Come on, have another go," he said, tossing the ball back at me. I had no option but to stand it up in the little dent again. I took four steps back. This time to hell with my feeble imitation of O'Gara – I ran up and whacked the ball as hard as I could. It soared up over the crossbar and between the posts. The groundsman gave me the thumbs up sign. I walked away, the cheers of the crowd ringing in my ears.

An event of more serious significance took place while we were filming the documentary. There may be only a thousand or so Jews in the whole divided country, but there still has to be a Chief Rabbi of All-Ireland, and a new one, Rabbi Gavin Broder, a young South African, was about to be installed. The ceremony was taking place in the Terenure Synagogue. The organising committee had decided that Adelaide Road had had its share of great occasions, and now it was Terenure's turn. In the past the high quality of Irish Chief Rabbis had borne no relation to the low quantity of the congregation, a fact obviously recognised by the pillars of the Irish Establishment who had come to the installation ceremony. The Papal Legate, the Catholic and Protestant Bishops of Dublin, the Chief of the General Staff, the deputy Head of the Garda, a host of other religious, civic, and diplomatic dignitaries, and the President herself. Mary Robinson's presence had apparently caused the organising committee hours of heated discussion. In an orthodox synagogue the women are separated from the men and sit in the gallery. Half the committee argued that it would be deeply disrespectful to segregate the President of the Republic. Naturally, on a Jewish committee, an equal number didn't agree, saying it was better to be disrespectful to a President than to God. Eventually a compromise was agreed.

On the day, President Robinson was escorted up to the middle of the front row of the women's gallery. The compromise was that she sat there, but between her husband and her military aide. It was like being in the royal box at the Opera, a perfect position for a President with a smile that could light up any synagogue.

From the third row back I had a rear view of the assorted dignitaries and realised that the Jewish ones all wore black yarmulkas, and the Catholics all purple ones. As the service was long and in Hebrew, there was plenty of time to ponder other parallels. Both faiths believed in a Messiah – the Catholics believing He had been already, the Jews that He was still to come. The Jews prayed in Hebrew, which most of them didn't understand, while the Catholics for most of the last century prayed in Latin, which they didn't understand either. Above all, both religions inculcate a fine sense of guilt. In a recent lecture on Joyce, I had heard Senator David Norris observe that, "If the Jews invented guilt, the Irish Catholics have turned it into an art-form."

The Chief Rabbi of Great Britain, Jonathan Sacks, must have read my thoughts. In his address he itemised how much the Irish and the Jews had in common – "long histories of persecution ... both demographically small yet with great impact on the world, a strong sense of history and identity, a love of language and literature, and, if I may put it bluntly, we are both great talkers ... both intensely religious, but with a celebrated sense of humour." He finished by making the Irish sound almost Jewish, and vice versa. The black and the purple yarmulkas nodded their ecumenical agreement. Then, as the great, the good, and the ordinary stood up to sing 'The Soldier's Song', one felt the Irish and the Jews should live together happily ever after, if only enough young Jews would stay put and reproduce.

The next day I was due to fly back to London. However, the Old Age Home managed to contact me just before I set out for the airport. Hilda had died that morning. By then deaf, blind, and arthritic, her life had become a burden to her. She was ninety-two, the same age as Deng Xiaoping, the Chinese President, who had also died that morning. I made arrangements for the funeral next day and phoned Ashley in London.

The Synagogue Burial Society is so efficient that there was little for me to do, except drive out next morning and collect Ashley from Dublin airport. The entire country was being pounded by gale force winds, and all flights were delayed. Eventually the arrivals board announced that Ashley's flight had been diverted to Belfast. There was no possibility now that he would arrive in time for the funeral, so I drove back to the cemetery at Dolphin's Barn. It had never looked bleaker, but a *minyan* of loyal Dubliners had arrived to ensure there could be a proper service, and the Chief Rabbi, of forty-eight hours standing, was there in his waterproof boots to conduct it.

Rabbi Broder chanted from the Psalms as we walked along behind the coffin to the grave. The wind, gusting at 80 mph, blew the rain horizontally into our faces. Umbrellas were blown inside out and abandoned. Yarmulkas were blown off and soared away over tombstones. I jammed a peaked cap on my head as the wind howled, the sheets of rain cold and cutting. It was the Irish-Jewish version of *Wuthering Heights*. At the graveside Rabbi Broder had to shout to make his prayers heard. Then it was the next-of-kin's turn to say *kaddish*. As Ashley's flight was still circling Belfast, I was on my own. I should have been able to recite it from memory through repetition over the years, but I didn't trust myself. Putting on my glasses, I opened the prayer book for the reassurance of the Hebrew text. It was like reading through a waterfall, the rain crashing against my glasses, the words indecipherable. I would have to do it blind. *Yisgadal veyishkadash shimay rabo ...* I intoned, as one shoe started to fill up. *Bolmor dee-braw kerosay ...* I was shortly soaked through, but the memory held out: *... shalom olanu val kol yisroel, vyimroo amen.* I had made it to the end, and we had buried Auntie Hilda, albeit slightly further apart from Minnie in death than in life, as we had carelessly forgotten to book an adjoining plot.

When their father, Tzale Ber (aka Bezalel Dov) Preuss had landed in Cork, this cemetery had not existed, there had been no President of Ireland, male or female, and certainly no Chief Rabbi. Now, in a mere forty-eight hours, as in some jumbled game of "Consequences", I had met the President and two

Chief Rabbis – and the Irish one now stood getting soaked beside me at the graveside. For a few brief, wet moments, all the strands had come together, but, sadly, there were no Prices, at least not Litvak Prices, left in Ireland. Perhaps, finally, it was time to write about them.

Sandycove 2002. The house is the same; only the author has changed.

21. The End?

In May 1999 Adelaide Road synagogue was sold for £6 million to a property developer from Galway. It has since been turned into an office and apartment block, with only the façade of the synagogue, as a listed building, retained incongruously amongst the surrounding glass and high-rise. The displaced congregants amalgamated with Terenure synagogue and there have been, inevitably, basic disagreements about what to do with the money. All agree that it should be used to aid and revitalise the community – but how? Some want to demolish the synagogue and start afresh. Others merely want to refurbish. Yet others, more ambitiously, want to put a community centre and a retirement home on the site. There is currently as much Jewish disagreement on the South Bank of the Liffey as on the West Bank of the Jordan. In any event, in 2001 Rabbi Broder returned to England and the more peaceful life of a college chaplaincy.

In January 2002 an almost identical cast as four years before assembled to inaugurate a new Chief Rabbi, Yaakov Pearlman. In the front row of the gallery was another President with another radiant smile, Mary MacAleese. In his speech the same Chief Rabbi from across the water, Jonathan Sacks, dwelt once more on the similarities between the Irish and the Jews, but this time his stand-up technique was sharper, his jokes punchier. With practice he was getting better at playing to an ecumenical Irish audience. There were the same prayers and the same anthems, only now there were fewer than a thousand Jews left in the country – Jews, that is, who are identified in some way with either the orthodox or progressive communities.

In Cork, Gerald Goldberg, at ninety, still goes to the synagogue when it opens for the New Year and Day of Atonement. Only now, instead of importing young Jews from Dublin, they bring over eight ultra-orthodox Lubavitch Jews from London to guarantee a *minyan*. And in February 2002, Freddy Rosehill opened the synagogue specially for his grandson's barmitzvah.

Adelaide Road synagogue. As a listed building, only the façade is preserved among the glass high-rise neighbours.

Stuart Clein remains the only Jew left in Limerick.

Alec Feldman now plays on the wing for High School First XV.

Presidents and Chief Rabbis still come and go. As do I, preferably via Dun Laoghaire. One of the suggested cures for insomnia is to relax and, in your mind's eye, go on your favourite walk. Mine is always along the harbour wall at Dun Laoghaire. And, in reality, I do it at least once when I am back

236

in Dublin. Walking outwards one has the view of Howth Head, walking back the spires of Dun Laoghaire against the backdrop of the Dublin Mountains. The multi-coloured sailing boats bob at their moorings. All around is Dublin Bay, hopefully still full of prawns and lobsters which I can now eat without guilt. I look across towards Sandycove and see the Joyce Tower and, in front of it, the house where we used to stay in the summer during "The Emergency". Halfway along the harbour wall is a telescope through which, if I focus it, I can see the window of the toilet where I locked myself in with Conan Doyle, coming out triumphant to go to Wesley. I also walked along here with my parents when my O-level results came through. My father gave me his great smile and took my arm. He was proud of me and pleased that I hadn't totally ruled out being a doctor en route to becoming another Chekhov or Somerset Maugham.

I have always found something comforting about the two welcoming arms of that harbour wall. They belong to that childhood world of rough wartime crossings, of sea-sickness and the relief of coming into harbour. There was also the sadness of seeing the mailboat, my father aboard, sailing out between them as my mother, brother, and I walked to the end, tiny figures waving. As a child I didn't know that endless departures were the theme of Irish history.

Now, when I am on the boat, sailing out through the open end of that horseshoe, I have the strange sensation of both going home and leaving home at the same time. My parents must have felt that way too on the countless times they passed this way. It is the divided self that haunts all expatriates and exiles. I seem to have inherited it. Even though my mother always said you must have somewhere to hang your hat, she herself ended up with at least two places. As for my own hat problem, I have finally resolved it, at least officially, by having two passports.

Acknowledgements

I would like to thank the following for their help or hospitality – in most cases it was both – in the course of my researches.

In Cork there is Gerald Goldberg, Freddy and Patsy Rosehill, James Roose-Evans and Hywel Jones, Gerald McSweeney, and Sally and George Phipps.

In Dublin, Gerald Davis, Dr Andrew and Valerie Woolfe, Joe and Debbie Briscoe, Ronan Gallagher, Dr Michael Solomons, Brendan Crowe, Jacqueline Solomons, Clare Duigan and Stephen Plunkett at RTÉ, and the extremely helpful staff at the National Library and the National Archives, especially Catriona Crowe for locating an invaluable file.

I am indebted to two books that were for a long time the only works on the Irish Jewish community: Bernard Shulman's *Short History of the Jews in Ireland* (published privately in 1945) and Louis Hyman's *The Jews of Ireland* (published by the Jewish Historical Society of England, 1972). There is now also Dermot Keogh's fine academic work *Jews in 20th Century Ireland* (Cork University Press, 1999).

Finally, in London, my gratitude to Professor Ashley Price for his medical advice, to Munro Price for his encouragement, and to Judy Price for her editing skills.